Contents

Acknowledgments	vii
1 Introduction	**1**
Tourism as a Solution	3
Historical and Geographical Background	4
The Emergence of Dahab as a Tourist Site	6
Contextualizing the Research Site	7
Reasons for Selecting Dahab as a Research Site	9
Outline of the Study	9
2 Framing the Relationships in Dahab	**11**
Masculinity	12
Gender Ideology and Perceptions of Women	14
Sexual Ideology: Dangerous Women	17
3 Methodological and Theoretical Approach	**22**
The Sample	22
The Research	23
My First Entry into the Field	24
The First Stage of the Research	25
The Second Stage of the Research	25
The Third Stage of Research	26
The Interviews	26
Applied Methods	27
Theoretical Framework	28

4 **'Urfi Marriage and Societal Control in a Global Context** 30
  Socio-Economic Conditions in Egypt 31
  Motives behind the Attraction to Dahab 34
  Dahab and Income Opportunities 36
  Marriage Difficulties in the Egyptian Society 37
  Dahab and Sexual Freedom 39
  'Urfi Marriage as a Solution 40
  Deviation from the Norm 43
  The Family 44
  The Society, State Control, and Regulations 45
  Religion 47
  Availability of Drugs 48
  Conclusion 48

5 **Constructing Sexuality, Sexual Health, and Risk:**
  Male and Female Discourses in Dahab 50
  Constructions of Sexuality 51
  Constructions of Health 53
  Perceptions of Risk 55
  Risk and Protection 58
  The Relationship between Health and Sexual Satisfaction 59
  The Main Actors 60
  The Stereotypical Views of Egyptian Women versus Foreign Tourists 61
  Agency and Desire: Who Is the Proactive Partner? 63
  Perceptions of the "Other" and the "Self" 64
  Globalization: Are we Heading There? 65

6 **Femininity and Desirability:**
  Foreign Female Discourses in Dahab 67
  Discourses on Western Masculinity 68
  Discourses on Egyptian Masculinity 70
  Western Femininity as a Site of Power and Privilege 72
  Desirability and Beauty 75
  Post-Colonialism and Modernity 77

7 **Conclusion** 79

  Bibliography 82
  About the Author 86

CAIRO PAPERS IN SOCIAL SCIENCE
Volume 27, Number 4, Winter 2004

Beach Politics
Gender and Sexuality in Dahab

by
Mustafa Abdalla

The American University in Cairo Press
Cairo   New York

Copyright © 2007 by
The American University in Cairo Press
113, Sharia Kasr el Aini, Cairo, Egypt
420 Fifth Avenue, New York, NY 10018
www.aucpress.com

Cover photo © Mitzi Buys, Dahab

All rights reserved. No part of this publication may be reproduced, stored in a retrieval system, or transmitted in any form or by any means, electronic, mechanical, photocopying, recording or otherwise, without prior written permission of the copyright owner.

Dar el Kutub No. 23750/05
ISBN 978 977 416 013 4

Printed in Egypt

Acknowledgments

I WOULD LIKE to take this opportunity to express my heartfelt appreciation to a number of people, without whose continuous support and motivation, this study would not have been possible. My deepest gratitude goes to Dr. Mona Abaza and Dr. Helen Rizzo for their encouragement and continuous friendship. They have always shared critical comments about my work and have been vital contributors to this study. This monograph also owes its immediate inspiration to Dr. Hania Sholkamy whom I can never adequately thank for her encouragement and intellectual guidance.

I am very appreciative to the support given to this monograph by Dr. Iman Hamdy, the editor of Cairo Papers. Without her patience, continual optimism and practical advice this monograph would have never materialized. I also take this opportunity to thank the reviewers of this monograph who gave me valuable advice and critical comments.

I want to express my gratitude to Dr. Samia Mehrez, Dean Ann Lesch and the Magda al-Nowaihi Graduate Student Award committee for the selection of this study for the annual award in 2003.

I owe many thanks to Dr. Nicholas Hopkins, Dr. Nicholas Ciaccio, and Dr. Nazek Nosseir for their sustained support to the research project since its early stages and for providing me with conference grants to attend and present the findings of this research in international conferences.

I want to express my utmost appreciation and thanks to my friends Dr. Shahnaz Rouse and Dr. Kamran Ali, who have always believed in my capabilities more than I do. Their continuous encouragement and critical feedback have helped me throughout the research project. I also would like to thank Dr. Julia Elyachar who has always been extremely encouraging and supportive.

I would like also to acknowledge a number of people who contributed in different ways to my research project and ultimately to this monograph. Dr. Mark Peterson provided me with guidance from my first day at AUC. I thank him for his valuable insights and sustained interest in my work. Dr. Nadine Naber is a crucial contributor to this study. I am grateful for her generosity with her time and thoughtful comments. I will never forget the constant solidarity and support of my friends in the Ssociology/Anthropology Department who have always been encouraging, cheerful and efficient in communicating not only with me, but with all the students in the department. Special thanks go to Ms. Aida Selim, Ms. Reem Mirshak, Ms. Dalia Adel, and Ms. Safaa Yousef.

I would like to extend my gratitude to my dear family and friends who have always been there when I needed them and helped me at different stages of this research. Special thanks to my father, Ibrahim, and Ahmed for their selfless support. I am also more than grateful to Regine for her sustained support, encouragement, understanding, patience and devoting her time to my work. Among the many friends who read and gave me critical comments on different parts of this work, I specially want to thank Tessa Farmer, Dalia Abdel Hady, and Amira Abdel Khalek, as well as Charlotte Crouch and Junko Toriyama for their help at numerous occasions. I am also indebted to Ines Lawicki, Mitzi Buys, Sabina Hostettler, and Susannah Beckert for their emotional support during frustrating periods of my fieldwork and for providing me with contacts and valuable material in the field. I also would like to thank Yasser Elwan for providing me with precious resources and for the inspiring discussions on colonial photography. A special word of thanks goes to my friends Silvia Winter and Jörg Twele for their continuing friendship and their valuable support throughout the years of my studies.

I cannot find words to express my gratitude to Laila Yehia, Ahmed Shadi, Omar, and Farah for their unflinching support and friendship. To them all, thank you for always being there.

The Egyptian males and foreign females in Dahab who shared their life stories, experiences, histories, and sufferings with me are the center of this study, but unfortunately they have to remain anonymous. My sincere thanks go to all of them for their time and also their support throughout the different stages of this research.

Finally, this monograph is dedicated to my dear professor Dr. Cynthia Nelson. Cynthia was, and still is, a very influential person in my own life and the many lives that she touched. From the time I knew her when I was a student at AUC until her death in 2006, and up until the very moment, I am still discovering new meanings, transcending old ones, and finding deeper substance in all of the lessons I learned from her. With all sincerity, I dedicate this monograph to Cynthia who was not only my professor, but also a dear friend who supported this study from the early stages.

Chapter 1
Introduction

IN RECENT YEARS, globalization has exercised remarkable influence over the social, cultural, economic, and geographical domains of our life. Ostensibly crucial was the role played by developments covering spheres of media, means of transportation and communication in the deterritorialization and emergence of a global world. Appadurai (1996) examines globalization in terms of mass media, projecting the argument that "[s]uch media transform the field of mass mediation because they offer new resources and new disciplines for the construction of imagined selves and imagined worlds" (Appadurai, 1996:3). He argues that people tend to construct imaginaries about themselves and the Other through media. These constructions characterize their interactions with one another and influence their relations.

Globalization has increased the mobility of many people allowing larger groups of people to afford comfortable traveling for business purposes, to find better employment prospects, or for leisure. The ease of mobility has given tourists the opportunity to indulge in a cross-cultural interaction which ultimately shapes their perceptions of the Other, the locality they visit, and also of their own selves.

Furthermore, the shift towards a global economy, adopted by many states, has its direct impact on the lives of many people all over the world. Global pressures and the establishment of a global market have forced many countries, especially among those belonging to the developing world to restructure and adjust their economies. These changes were often a result of an internal economic crisis, but in many cases the adjustment took place to meet external demands from international bodies such as the International Monetary Fund (IMF) and the World Bank. Consequently there has been a lack of appropriate advances in sustainable economic development, especially in providing job opportunities for young people. The failure of the state in creating the framework for economic prosperity has led to the development of negative stances and feelings of alienation among large groups of the population in different countries.

The social as well as economic developmental strategies adopted by many states have mostly affected people at the grass-root level who have resorted to different survival strategies in order to cope with the economic hardships as well as the social problems in their societies. Bayat (2000) argues that millions of people in the Southern Hemisphere of the globe who used to rely entirely on state services have now to depend on their own efforts to survive. He adds, that it is largely agreed that: "the economics of globalization, comprised of a global market 'discipline', flexible accumulation and 'financial deepening' has had a profound impact on the post-colonial societies" (Hoogvelt, 1997 as cited in Bayat, 2000: 534).

To overcome the socio-economic developments, people in many parts of the world have resorted to various kinds of informal and at times illegal forms of generating incomes, such as child labor, street vending, drug dealing, and begging. In recent years, technological advances have helped in creating new job patterns such as offering cell phone services in the streets for a little amount of money, a phenomenon that can be observed in many cities in Egypt. While some of these behaviors show forms of adaptation to the economic difficulties and current changes, other segments of the population have developed passive attitudes toward their governments and have created forms of resistance manifested in the emergence of new fundamentalist political and religious groups worldwide. The growth of these groups in many parts of the world – including the developed world, the Middle East, South Asia, Africa, and Latin America – is related to the extensive modern developments in capitalism, the cornerstone of globalization that has led to unequal production growth depending on region, class, gender, and race. It is also closely linked to job insecurities as well as income gaps. These movements have developed as people search for a secure identity in the face of fast socio-economic and cultural changes that lead to creating wide income gaps, changes in the family, women's status, and sexual morals (Keddie, 1998). However, the ruling governments have, by large, have fought these active movements and tried to destroy them for years, as has been the case with Islamic fundamentalism in Algeria and Egypt.

At another level, globalization has created new markets and secured job opportunities to many people around the world in domains like the tourism industry, which is one of the world's largest industries that involves not only cultural exchange through the influx of tourists around the world, but is also a major employment provider.

Tourism as a Solution

In view of the obvious boom witnessed in the tourist industry, this sector appears to be the solution for many people's economic woes. Accordingly, many young people all over the world seek job opportunities in the formal and informal tourism businesses in order to survive the pressures of the increasingly globalizing economies. Thus, at a time while some parts of the population have resorted to informal means to make their daily living in order to adapt to the rapid economic as well as social changes and others have developed negative stances toward their governments, a third segment has tried to find employment in the tourism industry, especially as "a pro-tourist position is held by many planners of marginal economies who look to tourism as a new way of making money" (Mac Cannell, 1999:162).

In the framework of the tourism industry, some people use their sexuality as a survival strategy by offering sex services either on a commercial basis, such as male and female prostitution as can be observed in some parts of Asia and Africa, or as the basis for other benefits that it brings for the ones involved. The latter type of sexuality between men from underdeveloped regions and Western female tourists is the concern of this research. This type of sexuality is prevalent in many regions of the world, such as certain parts of Egypt, Morocco, Tunisia, Turkey, some South Asian countries, as well as other African and some Latin American countries. Over the past few years, tourism has expanded immensely (Waters, 1995), and through the tourism industries people have been able to construct certain perceptions of visited communities and localities, which often have a stereotypical character.

In the framework of tourism and as a vivid example of the situation described earlier, this research takes the locality of Dahab, South Sinai, as a case study and focuses on interactions between Egyptian men and foreign female tourists. It explores the reasons that urge underprivileged Egyptian men working in the informal tourist businesses in Dahab to seek casual sexual relationships with foreign women. It also attempts to clarify to which degree men and women are aware of the health hazards that can result from their behavior. It further explores the reasons that attract female tourists to a place like Dahab where sexual interactions between local men and female tourists are common. Finally, it examines how the female tourists perceive gender relations in Dahab as compared to similar relations in their own communities.

Historical and Geographical Background

The Oasis of Dahab is located in the governorate of South Sinai, which is famous for its mountains, valleys, attractive beaches, and the most precious coral reefs that exist worldwide. South Sinai is rectangular in shape and is about 17,000 square kilometers with distinct natural borders represented in the Tih Plateau in the North, the Gulf of Suez in the West, the Gulf of 'Aqaba in the East, and the confluence of the two gulfs in Ras-Mohamed which is located in the Southern part of the Sinai at the beginning of the Red Sea. Several valleys run between the mountains of South Sinai connecting its eastern and western coasts, some of which are easy to drive through, while others are difficult to access except by camel, donkey, or on foot (Lavie, 1990).

Lavie (1990) explains that rain in South Sinai is scarce and little; however, there are certain times during the year when this part of the Sinai Peninsula experiences vast floods that may cause massive destruction in the area, uprooting trees, destroying roads, and drowning animals like camels, goats, and sheep. The majority of the land in South Sinai cannot be used for agriculture even with irrigation due to the inability of the soil to retain water, as there are no organic substances among the sandstone and rocks.

South Sinai consists of several oases; the biggest is located in Wadi Firan. It stretches about ten kilometers and is mainly planted with palm trees and orchards of deciduous as well as tropical fruit trees. On the eastern coast of the peninsula lie the three large oases, Nuweba', Dahab and Nabq overlooking the gulf of 'Aqaba. The largest oasis in the western part of the peninsula is al-Tur, which is located on the Gulf of Suez. The monastery of Saint Katherine is at the center of the peninsula and has been continuously inhabited by Greek Orthodox monks since the fifth century (Lavie, 1990).

Prior to 1956, the presence of the Egyptian government in South Sinai was limited and as a result, the monastery of Saint Catherine assumed an important role in providing health care to the Bedouin community. It also served to link the Bedouins and the world outside of Sinai (Field, 1948, Forsyth and Sisson, 1964 as cited in Lavie, 1990).

After the 1967 war, Israel occupied the Sinai Peninsula and had control over it until it was completely retrieved by Egypt in 1982. Under the Israeli occupation, Sinai witnessed different stages of development. Lavie (1990) explains that the period from 1967 till 1972 was marked by a low level of investment to develop Sinai due to the prevalent hostility between Egypt and Israel as shooting and attacks were carried out on both sides along the Suez Canal. However, the opening of the road that connects Eilat with Sharm al-Sheikh in 1972 characterized a new stage that lasted from this

Chapter 1: Introduction 5

year till 1979 when Israel began to withdraw from Sinai. This road made it easier for Israeli investments to flow to areas in southern Sinai highlighting a new phase of development in the region. As a result, the tourism industry witnessed rapid growth in South Sinai and the Bedouins, mostly from the Mezini[1] tribe, were involved in the tourist businesses by arranging safari trips by camel or car as well as operating shuttle services between different parts of the region. Due to the new development plans,

> The beaches along the Gulf of 'Aqaba soon became an internationally famous pilgrimage site for naked sun worshippers, who came throughout the world. This brand of tourist was totally bewitched by fantasies about the Bedouin way of life and became the major clientele for paid-for Mezini hospitality. (Lavie, 1984 as cited in Lavie, 1990:68)

As an adaptation to the fast growing tourism industry, shanty settlements appeared in the oases of Nuweba', Dahab, and Nabq and huts were built for tourists using palm fronds, wood, and, cardboard paper.

In spite of the fact that the Bedouins in South Sinai benefited from the growing tourism industry, they complained to the Israeli authorities of the tourists' behavior and demanded that the tourists be instructed to wear bathing suits and shun inappropriate conduct. However, the Israeli authorities took no action and the military governor told the Bedouins "to make the best of it and learn to enjoy the show" (Lavie, 1990:222), while "[t]he tourists, for their part, saw no reason to wear clothes in "the wilderness" (Lavie, 1990:68).

After the 1973 war and the conclusion of the peace treaty between Egypt and Israel, Egypt regained Sinai gradually until the Israeli withdrawal was completed on April 25, 1982. After taking full control of Sinai, the Egyptian government took different steps to develop and promote it as a tourist destination. To achieve this goal, it paved two roads with asphalt, and the port of Nuweba' was built in order to facilitate tourist flows between Egypt and Jordan. In spite of the fact that Egyptians continued to run the tourist villages founded by the Israelis, the number of tourists started to decline and mainly backpackers—a type of tourists that the Egyptian authorities are not interested in—continued to come to the region (Lavie, 1990).

Meanwhile, the Egyptian authorities instantly responded to the requests of the Bedouins to regulate the tourists' behavior and erected signs on the

---

1 The Mezini is the largest tribe in Sinai. It lives in the southern part of the peninsula, such as in Sharm al-Sheikh and Dahab.

beaches of the South Sinai to forbid nudity, which consequently had an impact on the number of tourists coming to the region. In addition, new regulations and restrictions were imposed and the police continuously controlled the tourists and the Bedouins who dealt with them. As a result, the Bedouin community lost a valuable source of income and consequently complained to the Egyptian authorities in South Sinai and asked them "to ease the no-nudity and no-hiking regulations." However, their demands were denied and again "they were instructed to make the best of the new situation" (Lavie, 1990:223).

The Emergence of Dahab as a Tourist Site

During the Israeli occupation of the South Sinai, many tourists showed interest to experience the authentic and traditional Bedouin way of life. Upon their arrival to Dahab they always asked, "[w]here is the Bedouin village?" (Lavie, 1990:224). These demands encouraged the Bedouins to build an artificial Bedouin village for the tourists, which mainly attracted tourists of the hippie type who came to consume the "exotic" Bedouin culture, eat Bedouin food, drink Bedouin tea, and at times find a young lover.

In spite of the fact that the number of tourists in Sinai declined since the new regulations were enacted to stop nudity on the beaches, some tourists still came to enjoy the "exotic" Bedouin culture. Lavie (1990) quotes a Dutch tourist from Amsterdam who was in Dahab with a head cover that resembled a veil. Answering a question about the veil, she responded: "I heard it helps to attract a young Bedouin lover. When Israel was here, I bathed here nude, but what the guys seemed really interested in was my nose and mouth. So I'm covering them to make them more mysterious" (Lavie, 1990: 228).

Dahab became known worldwide for nudity, drugs, and as a hippie hang out. Many guidebooks wrote about the practices on its beaches. The lonely planet guidebook explains,

> *Dahab is the wannabe Koh Samui of the Middle East. Banana fritters and Bob Marley, stoned travelers in tie-dyes and shops with names like 'Laughing Buddha' offering tarot card readings – it's all here. Accommodation virtually on the beach can cost as little as E£5 per night and common is the backpacker who pitches up here for a night or two and ends up saying² on for weeks, if not months. (Lonely Planet, 1999: 492)*

---

2 Misspelling in original text, meaning: 'staying.'

Chapter 1: Introduction

Due to its reputation, it witnessed influxes of young Egyptian men who sought not only jobs in the tourism businesses but also relationships with foreign female travelers. Furthermore, the phenomenon that started under the Israeli occupation when foreign women came to Dahab to establish relationships with the "exotic, oriental" men has continued after Sinai returned to Egyptian sovereignty. Prior to starting my fieldwork in Dahab, in spring 2001, I met several foreign women who came to Egypt–more specifically to Dahab–and told me that they got married to Egyptian men as early as on the second day of their arrival. They also explained that casual sexual relationships and interactions between Egyptian men and foreign women take place on a daily basis and that *'urfi*[3] marriage is not limited to a few but is prevalent among most men who live in there. This phenomenon attracted my attention and raised questions about health implications resulting from the sexual behavior of Egyptian men and foreign women in Dahab, which was the impetus for selecting it as the site of my research.

Contextualizing the Research Site

Dahab is a small town situated on the eastern seaside of the Sinai Peninsula. It lies about 85 kilometers north of Sharm al-Sheikh and is one of the three big oases located on the Gulf of 'Aqaba. Despite its closeness to Sharm al-Sheikh with its well-structured, formal and up-scale tourism, Dahab has not yet been invaded by this type of tourism. It is still the destination of individual travelers and backpackers due to its cheap accommodation. Nevertheless, the local authorities are working hard to attract organized tourist groups and promote it as a tourist site on the tourist-map. They are introducing major changes to it, paving its roads and cleaning the beaches while a number of hotel chains are planning to build branches there especially in Laguna, which is located in the southern part of Dahab, where five-star hotels dominate the beautiful beach.

Dahab is divided into three main parts; Dahab city (al-Madina), situated in the southern part where a post office, two police stations, a public hospital, a telephone office, and a bus station are be found, in addition to a number of apartment buildings that accommodate the government employees working there. Al-Assalah is located in the northern part and houses mostly the Bedouin community who belong to the Mezini tribe. Al-Assalah has recently become an attractive site for many foreigners to buy property and build houses due to the cheap land prices in this part of Dahab.

---

3   *'Urfi* marriage is unregistered customary matrimony that can take place in a lawyer's office in the presence of two witnesses. This type of marriage is well known among western females in Dahab as the "Dahab marriage."

Al-Mazbat, the focus of this research, lies in the middle between al-Madina and al-Assalah and consists mainly of two roads parallel to the sea crossed by another two streets that connect them to the commercial center at the southern part of al-Mazbat. The majority of the tourist businesses, small hotels, camps, cafeterias, bazaars, scuba-dive centers, and safari agents are located in al-Mazbat and offer informal tourist services to tourists and individual travelers. Young Egyptian men who migrate from different parts of Egypt to Dahab looking for better job prospects are concentrated in this area and dominate the informal tourist businesses in Dahab. In addition, al-Mazbat has a small police unit as well as a language school attended by around thirty pupils, who are mostly the offspring of the inter-cultural marriages in Dahab. Al-Mazabat also has five pharmacies, two private clinics, a bank, and several small supermarkets.

As mentioned earlier, Dahab was reputed among Egyptians and foreigners for the availability of drugs and for its unusual sexual freedom. That is why it was sometimes called "Amsterdam of the Middle East."[4] However, the extensive presence of police that patrols the city regularly has limited these practices and made it difficult to market drugs in the area, which has changed this reputation of Dahab[5]. As for sexual practices, it has become common for Egyptian men and foreign women who show an interest in each other to solicit *'urfi* marriage contracts at one of the lawyers' offices in Dahab. This marriage is mainly used to justify the relationship between Egyptian men and foreign women and is used as means for the men to protect themselves from being accountable to the police, as will be explained shortly.

When I started to conduct my fieldwork, cafeterias and restaurants lined the beach of al-Mazbat, where guests could sit or lie down on pillows and cushions on the ground covered by carpets. These cafeterias and restaurants were built with palm fronds and were lit with colorful lights. Their loud music could be heard from a distance of one kilometer. However, during the time of my fieldwork (spring 2001 to spring 2003), Dahab witnessed rapid changes and over one night in the spring of 2002 the cafeterias were bulldozed and the local authorities ordered their owners that if they wanted to continue on with their activities, they had to provide the guests with chairs, tables, and wooden umbrellas. In addition, the main street that parallels the sea was cleaned and a small wall, about 50 centimeters high, was built along the beach to separate it from the main road. Moreover, the street – formerly a dirt road – was paved and turned into a pedestrian zone. According to a

---

4 http://www.egyptfocus.com/Dahab_here.html, visited April 25, 2001
5 http://www.egyptfocus.com/Dahab_here.html, visited November 22, 2002

Chapter 1: Introduction

member of the Dahab city council, these changes were introduced to attract a different type of tourists and to encourage up-scale tourism and tourism packages to the city.

Reasons for Selecting Dahab as a Research Site

Given the unusual prevalence of social interactions and sexual relationships between Egyptian men and foreign women in Dahab, I chose to focus my study on issues of sexuality and sexual health. In Egypt, the interactions between locals and tourists are prevalent in many tourist destinations such as Aswan, Cairo, Hurghada, Luxor, Sharm al-Sheikh and in many of the Western oases such as Bahariya, Farafra, and Siwa. However, only a few inhabitants of the mentioned tourist destinations work in the tourist businesses and only a small number of individuals are involved in casual relationships with female foreigners given the familial and the tribal control in these areas. It is worth noting that Dahab is considered unique in this regard since the majority of men working in it are immigrants who are not accompanied with their families. In addition, they are engaged directly or indirectly in the tourist businesses and interact with tourists on a daily basis. Furthermore, the absence of social control mechanisms, such as the family, allows for adopting behaviors that would be impossible to exhibit in the presence of these mechanisms as can be seen in places such as Luxor and Aswan. Moreover, compared to other places that are famous for their upper-scale and organized packages, Dahab, as mentioned earlier, caters mostly to backpackers. It has recently witnessed the influx of middle-aged foreign women who buy property and reside in the city and, in many cases, also establish sexual relationships with young Egyptian men.

Western female tourists have been traveling to Dahab for many years to enjoy the uniqueness of the place due to its charming nature, amazing sea, the beaches, and the mountains. In many cases Egyptian males approach female tourists seeking to establish relationships and as a result, many female tourists extend their visit to Dahab due to these relationships and in most of the cases, the relationship is legalized by an *'urfi* marriage contract. Often though, foreign female tourists are not willing to establish lasting relationships and limit their commitment to the geographical place of Dahab.

Outline of the Study

This study examines the relationships and the interactions taking place among Egyptian men and foreign women in Dahab. It highlights the reasons why Egyptian men and foreign women are attracted to this tourist destination as job-seekers and vacationers and explains how both Egyptian men and foreign women perceive each other. It also reveals the histories behind these relations by shedding light on the historical background.

In this context, Chapter Two will be devoted to examine the existing literature that deals with gender ideologies and constructions of masculinities, while Chapter Three will give an overview of the methodological and theoretical approach of this study. Chapter Four will then examine the economic difficulties and their impact on the youth in the Egyptian society, showing how *'urfi* marriages in Dahab are used as means to overcome these difficulties. It will further highlight conflicts the young men in Dahab have with their families and the authorities. Chapter Five will take the men in Dahab as the main focus to show how they construct their understandings around their sexuality, risk, and sexual health. It will also scrutinize the role that men take in the established relationships, and show how interactions with foreign women affect their views of their own selves, their society, and the Other. Finally, Chapter Six will further explore Western women's discourses on femininity and masculinity, highlighting their views of men in Western societies versus the men in Dahab. It will also examine the relationships in Dahab in light of the colonial histories between the East and the West.

Chapter 2
Framing the Relationships in Dahab

IN ORDER TO understand the intricacies of the relationships between Egyptian men and foreign women in Dahab, it would be useful to examine thoroughly the existing literature that tackles gender, sexual ideologies as well as masculinity issues, and also see the ways in which different cultures reproduce and reinforce stereotypical views of gendered behaviors as well as the distribution of gender roles. Moore (1994) explains that sexual and gender discourses view women and men as entities representing different standards of agency. She points out that Western societies view males and their sexuality as 'active,' 'aggressive,' 'thrusting,' and 'powerful' contrary to females and their sexuality who are perceived as 'powerless,' 'passive,' submissive,' and 'receptive' (Moore, 1994:50). According to her, the importance of gender discourses does not stem from the fact that they provide precise accounts of social practices and experiences, rather they engender women and men as beings who are 'defined by difference.' "These forms of difference are the result of the working of signification and discourse, and when brought into play they give rise to the discursive effects that produce gender difference itself, as well as gender categorizations" (Moore, 1994:51).

I will first explore how masculinity is constructed in a way that favors men by granting them certain privileges in the society. I will further investigate the gender ideology and the ways women are positioned in their societies and the attempts of some feminist discourses to adopt a gender model that is distinct from the male one in their struggle for equality. Finally, I will look at male sexual ideologies and how men in some societies fear women and their sexuality.

Masculinity

A great impact on the differentiation between males and females and in assigning certain gendered roles to both groups comes through culture. However, culture is a human product. Geertz argues that, "man is an animal suspended in webs of significance that he himself has spun" (Geertz, 1973:5), and describes culture as these webs of meaning which human beings produce and live in after the process of socialization.

In early childhood, humans are socialized during a long process in order to shape what is considered masculine men and feminine women. Gilmore (2001) explains that all societies differentiate between males and females and provide "institutionalized sex-appropriate roles for adult men and women," rather than permitting flexible behavior patterns in gender and sex roles (2001:207). However, the notions of masculinity and femininity change from one culture to another and over time. Connell (1998) clarifies that different types of masculinity "can be found within a given cultural setting or institution" (Connell, 1998:4). This can be observed within families where elder men are considered more masculine than younger ones or in institutions such as schools, workplaces, and the military where different types of masculinities are prevalent. Furthermore, some cultures require of men to go through initiation rituals to affirm their masculinity. In this connection, Gilmore (2001) drives the example of men on the Turk Island in the South Pacific who should grapple with dangerous situations such as going on deep-sea fishing trips in small boats. In such situations, retreat equals being effeminate.

In the Arab culture, constructions of masculinity and femininity have affected people's preferences by privileging sons over daughters. The boundaries drawn between masculine males and feminine females have materialized and stabilized over time to produce patriarchal dominance over women. The enactment of these masculine notions requires of men to behave in certain manners and take actions that are not available in many cases for women. Entering the public sphere, being the breadwinner and socializing with other men are means through which men assure their masculinity as can be observed in many parts of the Middle East. In his study among a group of Lebanese men, Gilsenan argues that men have to have jobs in this community in order to reaffirm their manhood since 'sleeping in the house,' (Gilsanen, 1996:282) which means staying at home without a job, is primarily linked to women. In this community, masculinity is integrally connected to acquiring a job, money, and servants.

Touching upon the notion of masculinity among the Glendiot men in Crete, Herzfeld (1985) points out how this community is based on the

Chapter 2: Framing the Relationships in Dahab

superiority of men versus the subordination of women who are not allowed to enter into certain situations that are the monopoly of men. The issue is further compounded by the strict hierarchal system which allots inferior status to anyone who is not a Glendiot Cretan, including outsiders and enemies. A sign of manhood is to keep one's head up among this group. Being a man dictates actions that involve resistance to the government and authorities, such as carrying out certain interactions with the rest of the group or with other groups. These interactions are confined to men while women cannot or are not supposed to follow suit. His argument is intensified by stating that women in the eyes of the community are considered at the same level with sheep; both are kept in one place, like the case in *harem*, and both are conceived as objects.

To secure manhood status, men of the Glendiots in Crete, similar to those on the Turk Island, have to go through dangerous situations. The fact that they have to steal sheep, raid, and go in adventures with other men helps them become men and also make friends by establishing alliances with the victims who acknowledge the daring skills of the young men. Such interactions take place to satisfy their needs of manhood as Hertzfeld claims "one must be good at being a man" (Hertzfeld, 1985:47). One can observe that the acts described by Herzfeld in Crete help men to boost their masculinity in order to be accepted by the rest of the group as hyper-masculine men.

In the Egyptian society, where male dominance is prevalent, men have to be 'men' and 'act like men.' Proving their masculinity is a daily basis that comes about by facing challenges, being the breadwinners, protecting the family's honor, as well as entering situations that might endanger their lives.

It is interesting to observe the variation in patterns of masculinity in different parts of Egypt. For example, men in Upper Egypt are assigned a hyper-masculine attribute when compared to men from other regions. The variation in patterns of masculinity is engendered according to class, religion, the geographical location, as well as the historical context. Blackman's account of (1927) hand tattooing among males in Upper Egypt indicated a ritual that drives men into manhood, a custom that is not practiced nowadays.

As male dominance is stressed, men are expected to show consideration of women's sexual desires, which they should try their best to satisfy. This affirms males' masculinity and maintains their dominance over their female partners. A man's failure to meet the sexual needs of his partner might lead the woman to seek sexual satisfaction with other men, which would imperil his masculinity, his position as a 'man' in the society, which would eventually stigmatize him cause social problems. These issues as well as dominant gender ideologies will be discussed in the next sections, which will assist in understanding the motives behind foreign female attractions to men in Dahab as well as comprehending the male behaviors and their actions within the relationships they establish with female tourists.

Gender Ideology and Perceptions of Women

As explained earlier, females and males go through socialization processes and rituals that shape their roles within the family, the culture, and the society they live in so that they follow specific regulations. Further, these roles require certain behaviors that are associated with the masculine and feminine conduct. As prevalent in many cultures, the socialization processes that women and men experience frame women's status in the society so that they occupy a subordinate position compared to men who are expected to be the dominant actors. Within the family, men and women perform the roles that they have acquired throughout their childhood as teenagers and, later on they model these roles and pass them on to their children (Botman, 1999). Furthermore, the different state laws and policies as well as customary interpretations of religions legitimize the socialization process and the gender roles prescribed for both females and males (Hoodfar, 1999). In Egypt, this can be easily observed in citizenship and custody laws, which are mainly enacted by men and show patriarchal forms of dominance (Botman, 1999). Moreover, the differentiation between genders is very prevalent and can be observed in daily life Rugh (1988). In order to gain respect, females' commitment to their homes dictates certain societal regulations for them represented in dress code. In certain parts of Egypt, women have to dress in black in order to be able to move out of their homes, while men are able to move freely in the public sphere. Furthermore, their mobility is restricted by having to be accompanied by an adult male relative.

Historically, developments in sciences, written mostly by men, have contributed to reinforce the submissiveness of women. Sherry Ortner's approach to female subordination is based on the assumption that the female's body is genetically and biologically created for reproductive functions. In her article "Is Female to Male as Nature Is to Culture?", Ortner (1974) relates the inferior position that women occupy in their societies to particular interpretations of biological factors which operate within the framework of culture. She explains that the universal subordination of women is based on the society's perceptions of them to conform to specific biological and genetic roles. Female bodily functions such as menstruation and delivery are strongly associated with nature, while men are considered to be cultural beings since they are closely linked to their actions. Ortner criticizes the culturally constructed

Chapter 2: Framing the Relationships in Dahab

associations between women and nature versus men and culture. She argues that women are not "any closer (or further from) nature than man—both have consciousness, both are mortal" (Ortner, 1974:87). Ortner's argument is that the cultural subordination of women in all societies needs to be explained since a universal inferiority, which only differs in its particular appearance must have a universal answer. Furthermore, Botman (1999) explains that gender relations are socially and culturally constructed rather than biologically determined. She adds that gender is characterized by social and cultural views, attributes, and manners that are designated by the society.

These gender differentiations are very obvious in many cultures. The traditional stereotypes directed at females and males have served to justify and rationalize the differentiation between women and men and the different expectations from them as well as assigning them different roles based on their sex. Smith (1994), in her study on Guatemala, explains how Maya women are expected to maintain the cultural identity through dress, language, and specific behaviors, while men from the same ethnicity do not have to adhere to the same regulations and often are not apparently different from men from the same class but a different race. She closely relates between gender, class, and race, highlighting that women are the guardians of pure blood; therefore, women from the upper classes are supposed to remain virgins until marriage and their marriage is not supposed to take place outside of their class in order to maintain the pure lineage. Similarly, she argues, men are expected to marry from the same race and class. However, it is acceptable for them to have multiple sexual relationships with women from different classes and various ethnicities. The indication here is that men are the community's privileged partners since they are entitled to actions and behaviors not acceptable from women.

The oppression of women throughout history and the dominant position that men occupy resulted in the emergence of a feminist struggle to fight and stop this domination and to further expand women's rights. This struggle has a long history that can be traced back to the late eighteenth century (Giddens, 1993). However, some trends of the feminist movement have adopted a male model in their debates, a model that has been subject to many critical examinations by other feminists. Seeing women's situation as different from that of men, Kristeva (1986) proposes a gender theory that is not based on the oppression of women and their submissiveness to men. She gives a critical analysis of feminism by shedding light on the historical background of gender relations, arguing that in past cultures women occupied socially high-rank positions, often related to their reproduction function, which was seen as an advantage that they possessed. That is partly why in many cultures, people used to worship female divinities. However, through historical developments men gained more rights that gave them the capability to control women and their reproduction function through different institutions such as marriage. She further examines the Judeo-Christian influence on gender and sheds light on the creation of the world as described in the book of Genesis by giving an analysis of the creation of Adam and Eve, which has given way to the belief that the inferior position of women was mentioned in the scriptures. She further points out that this inferiority is entrenched both in the Old the New Testaments. She explains that Judaism undermines the position of women, gives more agency to men, and draws a clear line between males and females by creating a system based on male domination and sexual difference. As for Christianity, it not only enforces gender differences, but also adds new aspects of male hegemony by stressing the importance of female virginity. It places a special emphasis on repressing women's psychological and physical needs, such as motherhood since it is considered a pleasure of the 'maternal' body. In such system of domination, women are denied their rights to any bodily pleasures while motherhood must be subject to fatherly control.

Kristeva's analysis of the position of women in Judaism and Christianity serves to trace their influence on the Western culture in order to form an understanding of femininity and sexual difference. She adopts a critical approach towards the lower status and reduced role of women compared to men as indicated in the discourse of the two religions. She further claims that these religions have shaped the feminist movements' agendas in the West. It is worth noting that due to the oppression of women, many feminist activists around the world favored adopting a male model in order to gain their rights to be equal to men. Kristeva rejects this approach and suggests that feminists should develop a new and homogenous approach to femininity.

In her book *Passion for Difference,* Moore (1994) attempts to problematize gender theories by offering more challenging dimensions to the issue of gender and sex. Instead of the agreed upon model that gender is socially constructed and sex is biological, Moore suggests that biological differences are historical. She suggests the adoption of the Foucauldian model that proposes the social construction of sex. Moreover, she uses a more pragmatically oriented theory, which is the "standpoint theory," suggesting that women differ in their viewpoints from men and that certain groups of women also have different perspectives. Moore argues that this theory honors groups over individuals. However, she also points out that all of us have different experiences and understandings of various cultural issues, symbols, and institutions. Thus, this can be a starting point for men and women, in particular, to understand their position in the society and act accordingly so as to develop a suitable standpoint for themselves. She clearly agrees with Kristeva that feminists should adopt a model that is derived from their own position in the society which differs from that of males.

Touching upon issues of identity and gender, Moore argues that both issues have been discussed separately in anthropological research although psychoanalytic theories of the development of self, which anthropology draws largely on, are based on sexual differences. She points out that the leading Western discourse of the self is that of the sensible, self-determining, and unitary individual, but criticizes this perception since many people do not see themselves and their actions as being rational all the time. In addition to the dominant discourse, other models have evolved. Moore illustrates that anthropologists have used the dominant model to view themselves and their work, but she calls to analyze and reflect critically upon the underlying discourse or folk models that are used in academic theories.

Cross-cultural research has shown that different local models of self and identity exist depending on the cultural environment. However, there are universal traits of identity such as self-awareness, the capacity to discern between self and others, and the consciousness of self-continuity. Moore explains that the model of the self in anthropology is often viewed as gender neutral, which means that the self evolves ontologically before the distinctiveness of gender. This concept implies that the self is present at the center of the person at a time before the socialization process even starts. She argues that, anthropologically, the essential factor that defines identity is the physical embodiment. Referring to the work of Judith Butler, she points out that the Western models of gender are important for the formation of the self in light of the psychoanalytic discourse since it is based on sexual difference of male and female. In feminist theory, however, gender and sex are viewed as two different entities and that gender is socially constructed. However, Moore criticizes the feminist argument as reproducing the same supposition that it derives from Western models, which are not universal as shown by research. This is therefore a challenge against the underlying understanding in the Western conceptualization of the relation between self, identity, and gender, especially with regard to the understanding of the fixed essence of gender at the center of a person.

Sexual Ideology: Dangerous Women

In spite of the common belief regarding women's physical weakness and their inferior position in society, women are feared as a threat to men and to the moral conduct in many cultures. As a result, in many cases women are deprived of access to the public sphere. They are mostly confined to the private domain in order not to cause any disturbance to men. The analysis provided by Brandes (1981) of the San Blas community's sexual ideology in Spain shows that men's fear of women stems from the belief that women's sexuality is powerful to the extent that they can always obtain what they desire, which triggers a sense of insecurity among men. Moreover, the potency of female sexuality poses a danger to men and to their masculinity. Therefore, women have to be controlled. In addition, females' sexual conduct can be a threat to the masculinity of their kinsmen and can jeopardize their position in the community. To give more validity to their beliefs, men refer to the Bible in order to segregate women, invoking Eve's seduction of Adam to taste the forbidden fruit. Women are portrayed as the evil that jeopardizes men's lives since they are the consumers of their semen, which is a finite substance that is depleted by women, curtailing men's vitality, vigor, energy, and consequently leads to their death.

Similar to the sexual ideology in San Blas, Botman (1999) explains that the control of women's sexuality by men is carried out in two manners. The first is by force exemplified in rape and pornography; the second is by laws that limit their rights over abortion and birth control. As far as Egypt is concerned, women's sexuality is viewed as potent powers that must be controlled by certain practices, such as segregation and clitoridectomy.

Citing Qasim Amin, Mernissi (1987), argues that women are not pleased with their oppression but have to accept it only because they are convinced with the widely believed fear in society that they and the way they behave could cause "*fitna*, disorder or chaos" (Mernissi, 1987:31). She further notes that *fitna* also stands for "a beautiful woman—the connotation of a *femme fatale* who causes men to lose their self-control" (Mernissi, 1987:31). In this regard, Amin uses this word to refer to the confusion caused by sexual disorder that is commenced by women. He concludes that if men are the weaker sex then they are the ones who should be controlled, protected and, consequently, they should be the ones who adopt the veil.

Mernissi also examines the work of Imam al-Ghazali where he suggests that the Islamic society suffers from a contradictory attitude regarding sexuality. This contradiction stems from the theories of female sexuality as argued by the "explicit theory" and the "implicit theory." Mernissi argues that the explicit theory supports the current common belief that men are aggressive in the way they deal with women and that females play a passive role She adds that the implicit theory as "driven far further into the Muslim unconscious, is epitomized in Imam Al-Ghazali's classical work. He sees civilization

Chapter 2: Framing the Relationships in Dahab

as struggling to contain women's destructive, all absorbing power" (1987:22). Therefore, women have to be controlled in order to protect men and allow them to concentrate on their social and religious obligations.

Mernissi highlights that the implicit theory of female sexuality as understood from Imam al-Ghazali's interpretation of the Quran, "casts the woman as the hunter and the man as the passive victim" (1987:33). She also cites Qasim Amin's work which argues that women's ability to control their sexual desires is stronger than men's and as a result women's oppression is used as means to guard men, not women.

According to Mernissi, al-Ghazali's reading suggests that the social wellbeing of the society is based on the satisfaction of women's sexual needs. Therefore, it is a social obligation of males to satisfy women's sexual desires in order to protect the society from *fitna*. She adds that the security of the society is linked to the fact that women limit their sexual relations to their husbands because this prevents chaos in the society.

In Egypt, impotence and sexual disorders are feared among large groups of men. Wassif and Mansour (1999) argue that men view women's sexual desires as strong. The power of females' sexual desires is reduced by female genital mutilation to ensure male domination and a harmonious marriage life. There is a prevalent belief among Egyptian men that female sexual desire is twenty-four times stronger than male sexual desire. Therefore, female genital mutilation is used as means to limit female desires and protect the society from their deviation.

Furthermore, Ali (1996) depicts that impotence and sterility cause a great deal of unrest among men in Egypt. He argues that curses and magic are usually held responsible for impotence. One can observe that men's views throw the blame for sexual disorders on something alien to them. According to Ali, the fear of the potent sexual desires of women and the common belief that women require longer intercourse to reach orgasm encourage men at times to use medications to ensure the satisfaction of their wives, fearing that an unsatisfied wife might search pleasure with other men, which consequently could cause *fitna*. He adds that worries about women's unfaithfulness lead their husbands to limit their movements. In some cases, this is also the reason behind many types of domestic violence. Hence, men fear female desires and attempt to satisfy them to ensure their masculinity since a man who is unable to satisfy a woman is effeminate or gay (Wassif and Mansour, 1999).

Egyptian men also think there is a link between food and sexual conduct. They believe that certain types of food, such as meat, enhance the functions of the body and ensure better sexual performance (Ali, 1996). Quoting one of Ali's informants highlights how men link their bodily disorders to the quality of food, "Without meat and with all these worries I ejaculate in a few minutes, whereas the rich man can keep his erection for half an hour and satisfy his spouse" (Ali, 1996:106). Men's discourse on curses, magic, and the quality of food needed for healthy sexual performance shows how they construct themselves and their bodies as vigorous and how they tend to blame external causes for their sexual malfunctions and disorders.

Furthermore, men's fear of women is not limited to their sexual desires. In many cultures they are perceived as impure, especially during times of menstruation. Gutmann highlights this issue in his study of Mexico in which he argues that men show special concern not to touch their female partners when they have their menstruation. To further distance themselves, they attempt to avoid eating food cooked by women who are menstruating. He explains that there is a common belief among the group he studied that if menstruation blood comes into the food or drinks of a man, he "will automatically fall under the spell of the woman whose menstrual blood he has ingested" (1996:122). Men in Egypt echo this belief as they consider menstrual blood as deadly.

Moreover, Mernissi (1991) explains that religious teachings draw a great deal of attention to the body and its functions such as secretions, fluids, and orifices, which children must learn about, pay attention to, and also control. She adds that Islam requires from both males and females a specific ritual of purification after intercourse, while a woman has also to wash her whole body according to an exact ritual after menstruation. She further explains that "Islam stresses the fact that sex and menstruation are really extraordinary (in the literal meaning of the word) events, but they do not make the woman a negative pole that 'annihilates' in some way the presence of the divine and upsets its order" (1991:74).

Given the fact that menstruation is not considered negative in Islam, it is allowed for spouses to enjoy each other's bodies when the woman is menstruating as long as they do not have an intercourse. However, some current religious books consider women as a source of enjoyment to men, which highlights widespread popular beliefs about women in religious disguise. Analyzing the section that deals with physical contacts with women during menstruation in the book *Ahkam al-Shari'a al-Islamiya* written by former Grand Sheikh of al-Azhar Gad al-Haq (1997) in conjunction with a group of medical doctors and scientists shows how common constructions of women as a source of pleasure for men are prevalent in current religious beliefs. In this section, the book explains how a man can enjoy the body of his wife during menstruation, referring to her body only as a source of enjoyment for the man regardless of her own pleasure. It states that a man has the right to enjoy his partner's body except for having intercourse with her. It also recommends that the man should cover her between the navel and knees, which is an implicit reference that this part of the body is impure and should not be touched or enjoyed compared to the rest of the body.

Chapter 3
Methodological and Theoretical Approach

THE RESEARCH WAS conducted during several extended visits to Dahab over the course of two years between 2001 and 2003. In the early stages of the research, my intention was to focus on sexuality, risk, and sexual health-related issues. However, given the intricacy and the nature of relationships between Egyptian men and foreign women in Dahab, other issues arose in the research such as masculinity, femininity, gender relations, colonial, and post-colonial discourses of sexuality between the West and the East.

The Sample

According to Adler and Clark (1999) choosing the sample means deciding which persons, establishments, and associations will be the center or the interest of the research. I focused my project on different groups of people, the first of which consists of Egyptian men who migrated from different parts of Egypt to Dahab in search for better job prospects in the informal tourist sector such as scuba-dive centers, shops, cafeterias, safari agents, and restaurants. The selection of this group was based on the fact that they have established different types of relationships with foreign female tourists. The second group includes foreign females who live in Dahab or those who frequent Dahab due to relationships which they have established with Egyptian men, as well as tourists who have casually formed relationships with Egyptian men, or in the form of *'urfi* marriage. Finally, the third group is composed of

Chapter 3: Methodological and Theoretical Approach 23

a lawyer who oversees *'urfi* marriage contracts between Egyptian men and foreign women, a doctor, pharmacists working in the area, and an employee at the city council.

The sample of my research is selected according to the Non-probability Sampling method and alternated between the Snowball Sampling method and the Convenience Sampling method.

The Research

My research in Dahab focuses on *'urfi* marriage, sexuality, sexual health, and risk as well as on the discourses of masculinity, femininity, and desirability among a group of Egyptian young men and foreign women.

In the part of the research that focuses on *'urfi* marriages, health, risk and sexuality among Egyptian men and foreign women, I attempt to reveal how the men and women in Dahab construct their understanding of their own sexuality, health, and the risks related to their sexual behavior. I also investigate how in the cultural context of tourism and class struggle in Dahab, *'urfi* marriages and sexuality emerge as counter-cultural strategies for surviving poverty in Egypt in the face of an increasingly globalizing economy. I also look at how direct contacts with foreigners have affected the Egyptian men's perceptions of the 'Other', their own selves, and the hegemonic culture of the Egyptian society. Furthermore, health issues are discussed and geared toward understanding the power struggle within the casual relationships established between Egyptian men and their foreign partners.

In the section of the research that focuses on foreign females' discourses on femininity, desirability, as well as Western and Eastern masculinities, I concentrate on the reasons that attract foreign women to Dahab and to the Egyptian men there. This part of the research attempts to reveal foreign women's constructed views of Egyptian men versus Western men. Hence, issues related to desirability and beauty in the West as well as in Egypt are investigated. I further examine the gender struggle that emerges between the Egyptian men and foreign women, which I will discuss in light of colonial and post-colonial discourses.

The interviews with the lawyer who oversees the *'urfi* marriage contracts to sought to investigate the frequency of marriages, their legal status and the legal rights over children who result from such marriages. The interviews conducted with the medical specialists—such as pharmacists and a doctor working in the public hospital as well as in his private clinic in the area—were aimed at investigating whether there have been patients, Egyptian men or foreign women, who suffer from sexually transmitted diseases (STDs) or sought blood tests related to STDs. I also explore whether doctors working in the area or in the public hospital have been involved in awareness campaigns and/or try to inform the men of health risks related to STDs and how they are transmitted. The interviews with the pharmacists were geared toward investigating the kind of contraceptives that clients purchase and whether they are used by women or men. Finally, I interviewed a member of the city council to find out about the urban developments taking place in Dahab and the motives behind them.

My First Entry into the Field

It was in the early 2001 that I paid my first exploratory visit to Dahab. I spent the first two days in observation and note taking of different social situations that involved interactions between Egyptian men and foreign women. I could see many men and women sitting in the cafeterias lined along the sea, running conversations about the West, Egypt, relationships, and sex. Men displayed behaviors foreign to the Egyptian culture, hugging, kissing, and touching foreign women in public. I could also overhear men and women arguing about their relationships, others discussing a newly established relationship, or being in the process of establishing a new one. One of the conversations that grabbed my attention was related to a man trying to approach a woman who obviously had been in Dahab for sometime without being escorted by a man. He asked her about the reason why she is not with "a man" and her answer was: "I have no problem finding a man, I can have a man anytime I want; I am just waiting." Curiously, men seemed to invade the physical space of women whom they might have met for the first time by putting their arms around their shoulders or touching their bodies. Among the interesting incidents I witnessed was a man standing in front of the cafeteria where he worked, who stopped a foreign female tourist who was passing by. In the beginning I thought he was trying to draw a guest to his work place as it is customary among the men in Dahab to promote their businesses among the tourists. But they were involved in a long conversation. After a while he took out two cigarettes, offered her one, and kept the other for himself. He then took out his lighter and offered to light her cigarette while moving his head close to hers to light his cigarette at the same time. Afterwards, the foreign tourist walked the street parallel to the sea in front of the cafeterias several times up and down and always stopped for the man whenever she happened to pass by the cafeteria. Getting into more intimate terms, he guided her to a place to go where a few minutes later he caught her there.

Chapter 3: Methodological and Theoretical Approach   25

At this stage, I was able identify potential informants, to whom I could talk to about my research and asked for their help to find more informants. In addition, I also identified key actors who helped me and facilitated making contacts with potential informants in Dahab.

The First Stage of the Research

When I first arrived to Dahab I found a camp[6] in which I could stay during my fieldwork. During my stay, I observed the interactions between the men working in the camp and the female tourists. I also participated in their activities and evening gatherings for dinner and around fire, which gave me the opportunity to socialize with the two groups. It also was a good chance to introduce myself to the people in the camp and to explain to them the nature and purpose of my research. Since I established a rapport with the men working in the camp, I decided to start my first interviews in the camp. My first interview was conducted with the director of the camp who became one of my key informants, introducing me to other male and female informants. His stay in Dahab for a few years and his position as the camp director allowed him to be part of many social networks and to be acquainted with many people working in the tourist businesses, which ultimately gave him the opportunity to introduce me to many of his acquaintances.

As already mentioned, I limited the interviews to Egyptian men at the first stage of the research and only during the second stage did I include foreign women. This decision proved to be useful since my frequent visits to Dahab gave me the opportunity to meet some foreign women with whom I could establish a rapport. Later on, they helped me in my interviews by introducing me to other foreign females in Dahab.

I completed the data collection with the Egyptian men during several visits to Dahab. The age of the informants ranged from eighteen to thirty-five years and the duration of their stay in Dahab ranged from about two to fifteen years.

The Second Stage of the Research

When I decided to go back to the field in order to interview women, I contacted foreign females whom I met during the first stage of my research and asked about their willingness to take part in my study as well as to

---

6   All small hotels in Dahab are called "camps."

further assist me reach other foreign female informants who are or were engaged in a relationship with Egyptian men. During several visits to Dahab I was able to conduct my research with foreign women whose age ranged from twenty-three to fifty-five years and who have stayed in Dahab between two months and eight years. They were from different socioeconomic backgrounds and nationalities.

The Third Stage of Research

Given the sensitivity of the issues I researched in Dahab, I decided to postpone interviewing officials and professionals—lawyers, doctors, and pharmacists—to the final stage of my research. At the early stages, I was more concerned with understanding the relationships between the men and foreign women and their health implications as well as the culture of the locality of Dahab. However, I also realized that it was significant to include a lawyer, doctors and pharmacists in order to be able to further comprehend the health issues related to these relationships, their legality, and the legal status and custody rights over children.

During the third stage of the research I was able to interview a doctor working in the town, a lawyer who oversees the *'urfi* marriage contracts, and three pharmacists. In addition, I interviewed a member of the city council. I could reach this group through the contacts I had previously established in Dahab.

The Interviews

In-depth interviews were conducted with the research sample. I employed semi-structured interviews and used open-ended questions, which I modified when necessary. The research is based on person-centered interviewing, which has the advantage of giving the informant the opportunity to talk freely when she or he is in a private place far away from her or his own community and peers. According to Levy and Hollan (1998), it is important to interview the informants in a place isolated from his or her family, companions and social contacts in order to increase idiosyncratic responses since the presence of other people in the interview setting would alter the conduct and discourse into a public one that is socially appropriate. The advantage of the person-centered interview is that it gives the informants more space to talk about personal and private issues that they would not be able to talk about in front of persons they know, especially since the topic is sensitive and tackles issues related to sexuality and relationships. Therefore, even when

Chapter 3: Methodological and Theoretical Approach   27

my informants asked me to conduct the interview in the presence of friends, partners, or peers I insisted on a private setting.

Moreover, most of my male informants work for long hours. Due to this fact and realizing that their work is their main source of income, I gave them the choice to select the place and time to conduct the interviews. As for the female informants, they decided where and when to be interviewed. I also got the consent of the partners of those who were married or engaged in a relationship before I conducted my interview.

Applied Methods

Throughout my research I used the Non-probability Sampling method in spite of the fact that this method has certain disadvantages as argued by Wysocki (2001) who points out that the sample selected is not representative of the studied community. This argument is based on the fact that the informants take part in the study on the basis of coincidence and not in a representative manner and this restricts the researcher's capability to generalize the findings of the research outside of the studied community (Bailey, 1982). Nevertheless, I used this method since it has certain advantages, such as being financially affordable and relatively minor complexity, in addition to the fact that it can be done spontaneously with available informants (Bailey, 1982). Furthermore, I am more interested in understanding the actions of the people and their behavior than in generalizing the findings of my research in Dahab.

Another advantage of the Non-probability Sampling is that it is often used when the informants are easy to access or when they contact the researcher because they are interested in participating in the study (Wysocki, 2001). While conducting the research, some foreign women who live in Dahab contacted me expressing their interest to participate in my research and assist me in finding other participants.

To reach my informants, I followed the Snowball Sampling method in which members of the target group identify potential informants for the research (Adler and Clark, 1999). Due to the sensitivity of my research topic and the prevalent tension in Dahab as a result of the extensive presence of the police, this method was the most appropriate technique to reach my informants.

Finally, participant-observation was used in conducting my research in Dahab. As I mentioned earlier, I took part in many of my informants' daily activities. Besides, on different occasions I was asked for assistance in my informants' relationship conflicts and personal issues which also gave me some insights into the dynamics of these relationships.

Theoretical Framework

For me, symbolic interactionism proved to be the most appropriate theoretical framework for the analysis of sexuality, sexual health, and gender relations in the context of Dahab, which represents an intersecting point between tourism and globalization. It will be mainly used to understand the meaning that sexuality and health connote for both the Egyptian men and foreign women and to see how women construct their views about men in Dahab. Symbolic interactionism is concerned with meanings that result from interactions and not only from cognitive processes (Ritzer, 1996). Blumer (1969) underscores the fact that it is based on the actions of people toward objects and the meaning that these objects carry for them. He explains that the meanings are generated from social interactions with others, which are also adapted and changed according to the communicative course of action through experience. Thus, he believes that symbolic interactionism is a practical approach of a scientific study of human groups and their behavior. Methodologically, symbolic interactionism studies the topic of concern in its natural environment and is interested in the direct examination of the empirical social world.

Lear argues that,

> *Sex is a physical act with symbolic meaning that occurs through verbal and nonverbal communication; 'symbolic interactionism' has frequently addressed language and communication and thus maybe useful in studying the language of sexuality and its negotiation. (Lear, 1997:19)*

The ways in which sexuality and health are negotiated are important for this research as it attempts to give an analysis of sexual interactions between local men and foreign women in Dahab.

He further explains that, "[n]orms and values are also objects that guide interaction, existing as referents, which in interactionist terms are the internalized expectations resulting from experience in interaction" (1997:20). Understanding the norms and values is important in order to comprehend the interactions of people and their perception of each other. Since norms and values are the object of interpretation, understanding how people act according to them and the meanings they carry for people becomes imperative.

Finally, interactionism concentrates on two main issues: "the first is what is meant by the everyday life; the second is how one goes about studying it, the language one uses to describe it and the conceptual and methodological focus" (Schwartz and Jacobs, 1979 as cited in Lear: 1997:21). Symbolic interactionists refer to everyday life as a number of places located in the social time and space and the study of it involves groups of people in combination with settings, activities and the difficulties they face as a group. Symbolic interactionism attempts to identify emotions, reasons, and motives that shape the actions of people toward what they do and how they do it (Schwartz and Jacob, 1979 as cited in Lear, 1997). Sexual interactions and the accounts of the men and women in Dahab in addition to interpersonal relations and negotiations prior to as well as during relationships are the main interest of this research. Therefore, I strongly believe that symbolic interactionism offers the best theoretical framework in order to understand the actions, attitudes and behaviors of both Egyptian men and foreign women in Dahab.

Chapter 4
Urfi Marriage and Societal Control in a Global Context

IN THE EGYPTIAN society, marriage is one of the most important events in one's life. Hoodfar (1999) argues that marriage and having children are processes with which adulthood and self-realization are reached. Parents are always preoccupied with their children's future and their marriage. However, in recent years, marriage is often delayed because of different factors such as education, financial hardships, or familial circumstances.

Marriage patterns in terms of mate selection and wedding ceremonies vary according to region and kin relations in the Egyptian society. However, in many cases individuals do not alone determine the selection of their mates since relatives and family members always play a crucial role not only in choosing the partner but also in carrying out negotiations for both the male and the female (Rugh, 1988).

In Egypt marriage is the only "acceptable context of sexual activity and parenthood and provides the primary framework for the expression of masculinity and femininity and the fulfillment of gender roles" (Hoodfar, 1999:52). Marriage in the Egyptian society is a process that is regulated "by custom, religion and the legal system, which dictate the different roles and responsibilities for men and women" (Hoodfar, 1999:52).

In addition to the duties and responsibilities entailed in marriage, there are also the legal rights guaranteed by law for both men and women. Contrary to institutionalized marriage, *urfi* marriage is customary and unregistered. It was practiced until the emergence of the nation-state that required registering marriages and acquiring official marriage contracts. However, this type of customary marriage is being currently practiced in many tribal communities, especially when one or both of the marriage partners involved is under the legal age for marriage. Though *'urfi* marriage is socially unacceptable in modern Egypt, many young couples resort to it as a solution when they cannot afford to finance a registered, state-recognized, and socially accepted type of marriage. In most cases, *'urfi* marriage takes place secretly in the presence of two witnesses who, beside the couple, sign an unofficial contract as an evidence that the couple is married. In the context of the Egyptian society, Abaza (2001) explains that *'urfi* marriage can cause social and legal dilemmas once a conflict between the spouses arises. She further explains that since *'urfi* marriage is unregistered, it does not allow any of the partners to file a court case to prove the marriage status if the other party denies the relationship. In addition, it entails other problems especially when women file divorce cases, ask for alimony or marital rights, or when they want to prove their children's paternity.

In this chapter I will first examine the circumstances and conditions that have resulted in complicating marriage in the Egyptian society. I will also scrutinize the emergence of a subculture in Dahab and provide an analysis of how the extended use of *'urfi* marriage emerges as a survival strategy to overcome poverty and to legitimize the sexual relations that take place there. I will further examine other social aspects in the city and shed light on the conflicts that result from the men's behavior and their impact on the relations between them, their families, and the state.

Socio-Economic Conditions in Egypt

After Egypt gained its independence from the British in 1952, the Egyptian government adopted a socialist system and proposed new strategies of employment, education, and other services, such as housing and health care. The Egyptian population grew dependent on the state which pledged to grant education and employment to all citizens. However, the economic decline that plagued the country during the 1970s made the state shift to an open door policy. By taking this direction, the government aimed to pool foreign investments, a strategy with which the state intended to transfer the economy from the public sector—on which the life of the vast majority of the population depended—to the growing private sector (Rugh, 1988). In 1991, Egypt started the Economic Reform and Structural Adjustment Program (ERSAP) as a response to the economic problems and the increasing deficits in its budget and balance of payments (Korayem, 1997). However, in her study of this program, Korayem argued that it had a great impact on poverty in Egypt, which is measured by the number of households living under the poverty line. She stated that poverty increased "from 30.4% in 1981/82, to 35.9% in 1990/91 in the urban sector, and from 29.7% to 54.5% in the rural sector" (Korayem, 1994 as cited in Korayem, 1997:22).

The economic shift from the public to the private sector resulted in huge numbers of unemployed young people who were not assimilated in the new system. Practically, the new policies did not provide many people with plausible solutions. Therefore, as is the case with other countries where the sate economies were reoriented to fit into the new global context, the Egyptian people experienced economic and social hardships as they lost the state support. As a result, they have resorted to different strategies in order to solve their economic problems and to survive the economic hardship. Some of them have even developed a sense of alienation and a negative attitude toward the state and its policies, as can be observed among many of the young men in Dahab.

Many men in Dahab express their dissatisfaction with the regime's policies and relate their migration from the mainland to the town to the fact that the government does not provide jobs to young people anymore. Yasser, a 29-year-old man from Gharbia explains:

> *I have been here in Dahab for three years. After I finished my education, a high school diploma in commerce, I started working with my father in a small business. However, the economic difficulties that my family faced pushed me to travel to Jordan to look for better job prospects. But as I was not able to find a good job in Jordan I decided to come back to Egypt. When I heard from a friend that the possibility to find work is higher here, I decided to come. The opportunities and salaries here are better than in Cairo or elsewhere. The problem is once the young people finish their education in Egypt they face lots of difficulties. The job opportunities are very rare since the government does not employ anybody. Now employment is limited to certain people, those who have connections. Other than that there is no chance, which makes me question the importance of education since there is just no chance for employment.*

Mahmoud, 23 years old, from Cairo also shares Yasser's concerns:

> *I had to leave the university in Cairo and come to work here because my family is poor. I have six brothers and sisters. My father could not*

support us with his modest job in a factory. There were times when I did not have proper clothes to go to the university or to buy the books I needed for my studies. As a result, I decided to work in the tourist business. First I went to Sharm al-Sheikh, later on I came to Dahab because it is cheaper and the opportunities are better. I do support my family financially. I send them money whenever I can.

Mas'oud, 25 years old, who is originally from Alexandria and a graduate of al-Azhar University says:

The economic and political conditions were the main causes that made me come to Dahab. The fact that the unemployment rate in Alexandria is very high made me decide to come to Dahab, a tourist destination all the year round where better opportunities for work may be available. In Alexandria, I had a small business of dairy products, which I established after getting a loan. However, this business failed because my customers did not pay me their debts, which made me unable to pay back the loan. A friend of mine suggested that I should come with him to Dahab and use the truck, which I had originally bought in order to transport the products of my business, as a taxi.[7] I started working as a driver in a diving center, using my truck to drive tourists to diving spots. Later on, I moved to work in a camp, also as a driver. The state is not interested in helping young people. Recently, they have encouraged university graduates to apply for jobs in the government and promised that lots of young people will be employed shortly. However, I believe that the government is using this as a strategy to defuse the anger of the youth and to show them that it is really interested in doing something for them. However, the fact is that it will not do anything for them at all.

From these accounts, one can easily feel the sense of bitterness among those young people toward the state. Furthermore, the economic difficulties that men experience in general are not only related to work opportunities but also to their ability of starting a family and meeting the expectations set by society. As a result, they seek solutions for their economic difficulties in the informal tourist businesses and rely on relationships they establish with foreign tourists to overcome the woes of the increasingly globalizing economy.

---

7   It is common that trucks are used as a means of transportation in Dahab.

Motives behind the Attraction to Dahab

In contrast to common tourist patterns in many parts of Egypt, Behbehanian (2000) argues that tourists in Dahab go through many casual interactions with Egyptians who cater for their daily needs. Direct contacts take place in order to arrange for their accommodation, transportation, and safari trips to the desert. These interactions are the main opportunity for negotiating the establishment of sexual relationships. According to my informants in Dahab, some of these relations take place casually, while others establish a serious emotional involvement that might entail a *'urfi* marriage by one of the lawyers in Dahab. This marriage takes place only to justify the sexual relationship between the Egyptian men and foreign women who are not allowed to live together outside of wedlock since the police in Dahab harass unmarried couples and, in some extreme cases, push them to get married. As a result of newly established relationships, the length of stay of the involved female tourists is often prolonged. One of my foreign female informants told me that she was planning to go to Turkey after her visit to Egypt. However, she extended her stay upon meeting her Egyptian partner and signing a *'urfi* marriage contract with him. After spending three months in Dahab, she left to Turkey and then returned to her country.

Many researchers have examined the motivations of tourists' behavior. It has been suggested that many tourists are not motivated by the special qualities or attractions of their destinations, rather by the degree of a particular psychological satisfaction it contains (Crompton, 1979 as cited in Ryan and Hall, 2001).

Due to the fact that Dahab is an affordable tourist destination compared to many other places in Egypt, many tourists tend to extend their stay there beyond what was initially planned. This is another reason which gives female tourists a chance to interact with Egyptian men and in many cases establish sexual relationships.

When asking the male informants in Dahab about reasons that attract foreign women to Dahab, they only attribute that to the women's desire to get the sexual attention that they cannot find in their home countries given their physical unattractiveness. These women often do not meet the beauty standards of the West, which makes them sexually undesirable in their own societies. Hany, a 24-year-old man from Sohag who is committed to a *'urfi* marriage with a Scandinavian woman, explains:

> *The women who come here are lacking certain needs* ('anduhum na'as). *They come for the satisfaction of these needs through relationships with Egyptian men. There is always something wrong with them.*

Chapter 4: 'Urfi Marriage and Societal Control in a Global Context

> *They are either old, very fat, very thin, their legs are not pretty, or have something wrong with their eyes. These women cannot find partners in their countries and come here to meet men and satisfy the sense of being desired. I know that my wife is fat and before our marriage I had a story with another partner who had serious problems with her eyes.*

Sa'd, a 31-year-old man supports Hany's argument:

> *You can always find a problem with the women who come here that makes it difficult for them to find men in their countries. Just look around and you will see many old western women married to men at the age of their children. These women would never be able to find young men interested in them in their societies as it happens here. They mostly buy the men with their money and the presents they give them: today a mobile phone, tomorrow something different.*

In addition to marking foreign females as women who 'lack something'*('anduhum na'as)*, male discourse in Dahab constructs the image of female tourists who form relationships with men as women who seek experiences that differ from the ones they have in their own countries. They describe western men as lacking the qualities of manhood *(mish rigala)*. Therefore, they believe that these women come to Dahab in order to experience the real masculinity of Egyptian men. Hany articulates his views further by saying:

> *Many of my partners explained to me that women in the West have particular views of Arab men. They believe that we are more masculine* (rigala) *compared to western men. We also should not forget that the rate of homosexuality is increasing in the West and because of this it is not easy for women to find men in their societies. That is why they come here to seek men. It also seems that women in the West are free and have all their rights, but the truth is that they are oppressed (*mathoneen*) because they play the role of the male and the female at the same time and this is not easy for them at all.*

One can easily observe that in many of these cases men's attraction to foreign women does not stem from physical or emotional appeal,; it is rather based on economic advantages. By establishing relationships with women, the men find solutions to their economic problems and the women find satisfaction to what is described by the male informants as their deficiency.

A lawyer, who oversees *'urfi* marriages in Dahab, explains that most of the marriages in Dahab are based on economic benefits

> *In most of the cases, the men here marry foreign women with two things in mind: to leave the country if possible and to gain financial assistance by establishing a business, buying property or even a car. Otherwise why should a 20-year-old man be interested in a woman older than his mother?*

Dahab and Income Opportunities

The fact that tourists in Dahab largely depend on local Egyptians to arrange for their accommodation, food, transportation, as well as diving and desert trips has created different jobs that attract young men from all over the country who suffer economic and unemployment difficulties. Dahab offers young men a range of job opportunities in the tourist industry, working as shopkeepers, taxi drivers, or in diving centers, hotels, restaurants, cafeterias and cafes located on the seaside. As a result, these jobs allow them to interact on a daily basis with female tourists. Moreover, these informal interactions are a good opportunity for them to find an additional source of informal income by gaining some extra money for the services they offer to tourists through the commissions they receive from business-owners when providing them with customers. Saleh, a 24-year-old man from Mansoura, works in one of the camps and has been living in Dahab for three years. He explains that:

> *The relationship with any woman here starts as a business. By helping the tourist to arrange for a trip or to find a place to stay, we get commissions from the safari agents or the hotels for these services since we bring them customers.*

In addition, there are other means of generating income directly from the tourists when the men receive financial support from their partners. Monique, a German woman, 55 years old, explains that men in Dahab take economic advantage of the women and try to receive money from them directly or indirectly:

> *My ex-Egyptian husband always had a story to tell me in order to get some money. He always claimed that a member of his family—father,*

mother, or a brother—was sick and that he needed some money to send to his family in order to cover the hospital costs. In most of the cases, these stories make women feel that they have to help their partners, and in general they give them money to support them.

This explains what my male informants told me that marriage relationships are considered to be an opportunity to earn some money since most of the young Egyptian men depend largely on the money of their temporary foreign wives. During my fieldwork in Dahab, I observed a couple, a 27-year-old man married to a 38-year-old Dutch woman, to see how they manage their relationship. I noticed that during the visits of the woman to Dahab, she takes over the responsibility of all the expenses and the man does not have to take any financial burdens or spend any money during her stay. Furthermore, while she is in Dahab he moves in to live with her in a rented house, while normally he stays in a room with two other men in the camp where he works. Moreover, there are also other indirect benefits that men get from their partners such as gifts, clothes, and meals.

In addition, Behbehanian (2000) claims that many Egyptian men establish informal business relations with tourists as a stopgap measure to supplement an insufficient income, or as a way to support themselves while looking for employment. Hence, one can observe that the economic gains that the men in Dahab make through establishing relationships with foreign women help them to overcome the economic difficulties they experience as a result of the lack of employment opportunities and job insecurities. They also find solutions to their sexual frustration, which cannot be satisfied through an official marriage. Further, many young men cannot afford to get married or meet the marriage requirements imposed on them by the society, especially in light of the current socio-economic problems.

Marriage Difficulties in the Egyptian Society

In spite of the fact that Egypt has witnessed an economic hardship in the past few decades, marriage in Egypt has become more and more difficult. According to Hoodfar (1999) the social and economic modifications have exerted a great deal of pressure on men since it has given rise to more material expectations. Nowadays, there are many constraints that young people in the Egyptian society have to grapple with to be able to get married, starting from affording an apartment and furniture to buying the engagement present of jewelry *(shabka)* that the groom has to offer to the bride as well as paying the dowry *(mahr)* in addition to the expenses of the wedding itself and consequently the starting of a family. According to Khalifa (1995), financing a marriage is far beyond the ability of a great number of the Egyptian young men. He adds that the high housing prices leave the Egyptian young people with little space in an already over-crowded setting.

On one hand, marriage is required by the society in order for the people to be involved in any sexual relationship. On the other, it is made difficult by the society. This contradiction has given way to a counter culture that has emerged in different places in Egypt, such as Dahab. As young people began to look for alternatives to marriage, the *'urfi* marriage phenomenon became widespread among thousands of university students throughout Egypt, a phenomenon that has caused wide controversy in the Egyptian society in the past few years. They have also resorted to other strategies in order to discharge their sexual desires. Khalifa (1995) further explains that many young people look for dark streets to steal precious moments of intimacy with their partners in their cars, again a noticeable phenomenon in many parts of a big city like Cairo. However, the strategies followed by young people in the periphery still needs to be researched since they suffer from lack of public spaces compared to the ones available to those in a big city like Cairo.

'Urfi marriage is part of the cultural stock, although a marginal one. According to Abaza (2001), *'urfi* marriages have always been practiced on a small scale. She adds that the Grand Sheikh of al-Azhar issued a *fatwa*[8] to allow *'urfi* married women to have access to divorce. However, the controversy resulting from the *'urfi* marriages of the past few years took place basically because Egyptian females were involved. In a society where virginity is highly valued and a prerequisite for marriage, especially for females, sexual intercourse is only to be practiced within the wedlock. Contrary to this trend, the young men in Dahab establish sexual relationships with foreign women on a daily basis. However, this phenomenon has not caused any disturbance in the Egyptian society, unlike the social unrest that took place around the *'urfi* marriages among the university students, since the main actors in Dahab are men and nearly no Egyptian women are involved.

The material demands and the family's expectations of young men in the Egyptian society have exacerbated their anxiety regarding work and employment opportunities. Furthermore, the complicated marriage demands that men have to meet in order to get married such as affording an apartment, bride price and a list of household items has made it difficult for them to meet the requirements of marriage (Ali, 2002). As a result, the average age of

---

8 A *fatwa* is a formal, legal, and religious advisory that is mainly issued by official religious institutions.

marriage among both men and women in Egypt has risen and sexual frustration has increased due to the complications of marriage.

This situation is the main reason behind the appearance of the Dahab phenomenon. Khalid, a 32-year-old man from Sharqiya, verbalizes his concerns and criticizes the current circumstances saying that:

> These days marriage has become a commodity. The parents of the bride impose very difficult conditions as if they were involved in a business deal with the groom. They do not consider what kind of person is proposing to marry their daughter. They only want a person who has money. What can young men do in a society that deals with them in this way?

Dahab and Sexual Freedom
After the withdrawal of the Israeli troops from Sinai, the region has become the focus of the Egyptian government's efforts to develop tourist destinations in the area. Therefore, Dahab and many other places in Sinai have witnessed influxes of young Egyptian men looking for job opportunities.

During the course of my fieldwork, I had the opportunity to talk to older people who have been living in Dahab since the withdrawal of the Israeli troops and established businesses, such as shops and hotels. They explained that tourists, especially Israeli females, came to the Sinai to enjoy sexual freedom and establish relationships with Egyptian men exactly as they used to do with the Bedouins before the Sinai Peninsula returned to Egypt.

Being aware of these accounts and due to the prevalent lack of job opportunities in the Nile valley, the complications of marriage, and the widespread sexual frustration among young men, many of the Egyptian men migrated to Sinai not only to look for jobs, but also to seek freedom from the societal norms and to enjoy sexual interactions with foreign women that they cannot experience within the hegemonic culture of the Egyptian society.

In a society such as the Egyptian one, expected behavior is codified, starting from dress and body movements to the daily interactions of the people. Social contacts between males and females are very limited, especially in rural areas. In contrast, young men in Dahab articulate their content with the freedom they enjoy in the absence of the societal regulations. This can be observed in the behavior of the men in Dahab as Girgis, a 23-year-old man from Sohag who has been working in a restaurant in Dahab for three-and-a-half years explains:

> In Dahab, I enjoy the freedom which I missed when I used to live 'down there' (referring to the Nile valley). Here when everybody lies naked on the beach I can do the same. When everybody is having sex outside of marriage I can also do the same. There are no family restrictions and the society here is different. We have our own culture here.

Many of the young men I talked to attributed their migration to Dahab to their search for better job prospects as well as to the fact that the control system of the society is nearly non-existent. Mohamed, a 24-year-old law student from Mansoura, who works in a restaurant, explains:

> The nature here is very relaxing. It makes the person wanting to do things that people cannot do in other places in Egypt. People here can get very close to each other especially in winter when they physically seek warmth. That of course leads to sexual relationships which can hardly happen in other places due to the control of the society.

In spite of the fact that the social control mechanisms, such as family and the hegemonic culture of the society, do not exist in Dahab, other control mechanisms, such as the police authorities, set a limitation on the freedom of the young men there and their sexual interactions with foreign women. As a result, the men in Dahab adopt other strategies to justify their relations with foreign women and to overcome the obstacles created by the police authorities.

'Urfi Marriage as a Solution

Similar to tourist destination patterns all over the world, sexual activities in Dahab take place on levels varying from casual sexual relations, long term sexual relations outside of marriage, to short as well as long term sexual relations justified by an 'urfi marriage contract, which Pateman defines as the legal right of sexual possession of the partner's body (1988). Some of my informants explained that there are young Egyptian men who get married several times every month and sometimes every week to have access to women, since they are known for their sexual practices and targeted by the police as long as they are accompanied by foreign women. This fact has also been affirmed by the lawyer who says: "It is only a piece of paper for protecting themselves as long as they are with a woman. Once the woman leaves they can tear it up and marry another."

Chapter 4: 'Urfi Marriage and Societal Control in a Global Context

The local authorities acknowledge the *'urfi* marriage contracts, which can be obtained at any of the lawyers' offices in Dahab for about two hundred pounds. This is considered to be a small amount of money compared to the advantages that men gain from the relationship with a foreign woman. These advantages vary from using the women's bodies for free to enjoying economic gains and the possibility have access to western countries in case of legalizing the marriage contract. It is a well known fact that many foreign countries apply strict policies in granting visas to Egyptians but follow more lenient regulations in the case of marriage. In spite of the fact that the authorities approve of *'urfi* marriage contracts as a document to allow Egyptian men and foreign women to live together and also consider their children to be legitimate, *'urfi* marriage contracts are not widely officially recognized. For example, the *'urfi* marriage contract is not considered to be a legal document that could grant foreign women a residence visa to live in Egypt and their status remains that of a tourist. Monique explains: "I am tired of being here as a tourist; therefore, I took the *'urfi* marriage contract and went to the Mugama'[9] to get a resident visa, but the employee laughed at me and told me that this paper is useless."

The policemen in Dahab try hard to control the sexual relationships between Egyptian men and foreign women. They do not only harass them in the streets, but also might follow them to their lodging to ensure that foreign women do not stay with them. However, these actions contradict the legal situation in Egypt since there is no law that regulates sexual relationships outside of marriage and the only law that exists regarding extramarital sexuality, Law No.10 for 1961, handles cases of prostitution (Ali and Salim, 1992). Therefore, by acting in this manner, the police authorities exert power over the young people by enforcing a law that does not exist. According to the lawyer in Dahab some of the men frequently marry the foreign women they meet to avoid any harassment from the police. However, this strategy works on three different levels. The first one operates in relation to the police as submission to the current hierarchy and in response to the demands of the police due to their powerlessness. The second level concerns their own goals, which are the economic gains as well as the hope of leaving the country through a successful relationship with a foreigner. Finally, as a shortcoming, they lose respect in the hegemonic society by acting in an unacceptable manner and therefore the *'urfi* marriage works at their own expense. Hany has been trying to leave the country through a successful marriage with a

---

9 This is a government building at the center of Cairo, which has a section for registering and granting visas to foreigners.

foreign woman. However, he has not been successful. He summarizes his experiences saying:

> *After I finished my high school diploma I tried to find a job, but it was impossible. I worked with my father for sometime to support the family, but the job did not make me happy. A friend of mine brought me to Dahab and since then I have been working with foreigners. This has opened another dimension to my ambition, not only to find good work, but also to leave the country. I have entered many sexual relationships with foreign girls hoping that one of them would work out and end up with a legal marriage in order to be able to leave the country. I did not have to get the 'urfi marriage contract with most of my partners since I work in a camp, which is full of tourists; therefore, the police is not able to find out easily about my sexual relationships. However, I got married ('urfi) two times when I saw that the girls were a good potential for help. At the end, they always left me and went back to their countries when they felt homesick.*

Another case is Samir, a 22-year-old man from Cairo, who has been working in Dahab for two years, he explains how the men in Dahab look at foreign women as an opportunity to leave the country, he says:

> *In many cases, interactions with foreign women develop to more than a business relationship. In most of the cases, female tourists are seen as an opportunity to leave the country. The majority of the young people here think that the solution for their problems is to travel abroad regardless of how they reach their goal.*

Samir's dream is to go to the USA; however, he understands that this is very difficult and it has become even more difficult after the attacks of September 11, 2001. Samir now looks for alternatives to leave the country. The case of Samir summarizes many stories of the young men who live in Dahab. It also shows to what extent the young people in Dahab are willing to go in their relationships with foreign women in order to look for better chances abroad. However, during the course of my fieldwork, I observed only two cases where young Egyptian men could emigrate after legalizing their marriage to foreign women. One of them migrated to Australia and the other to Switzerland.

Deviation from the Norm

In Egypt, norms imposed by the society and reinforced by the family are very strict. It is difficult to violate the current traditions since the system of control is omnipresent. Moreover, the expectations of the society and the family are highly respected and young people adhere to them, sometimes more because social pressure rather than out of conviction. Rugh mentions that:

> *Poverty affects the composition of households, the carrying out of norms, the fulfillment of obligations, the quality of family relationships, the ability to deal with crisis, and the alliances it is necessary to make in order to survive. (Rugh, 1988:188)*

Accordingly, the majority of young men in Dahab use the deteriorating economic conditions to justify their behavior, arguing that the current circumstances do not allow them to abide by the norms of society. Furthermore, they explain that worldwide media has affected their traditional views. Mas'oud says:

> *You should not expect me to act in a certain way while I see that the whole world is changing around me. What we see on the Internet and television via the satellite channels makes us question our own society and traditions. Before, none of these forms of media existed. Therefore, today nobody should expect us to act as the previous generations did. Traditions work as constraints to my freedom, while here in Dahab there are no traditions that I have to adhere to; there is no control except for the police that tries to control the interactions between the young men and foreign women.*

Nasser, a 23-year-old man from Ismailiya, who came to Dahab eight years ago when he could not finish his school education, verbalizes his discontent with the traditions of the society:

> *Customs and traditions in a place where there are no foreigners are acceptable. But here, nobody adheres to such things due to the constant interactions we have with foreigners. We have reached a point here that nobody can control our actions; it is too hard to go back. Dahab is an easy-going place; everybody does what he wants. What is expected from me by the society is a routine; it is like a program that I have to follow.*

It is obvious from the previous accounts how the direct contacts of the men in Dahab with tourists and their exposure to different cultures have affected their behavior as well as their perceptions of the societal traditions and their own culture. However, the actions of the men in Dahab and their different life style have resulted in conflicts with their families, the police authorities, and sometimes the Egyptian society as will be explained in the coming sections.

The Family

In spite of the fact that Dahab is well known to have a subculture, which is not accepted by the hegemonic culture, some of my informants explain that their families do not oppose their work there. However, the majority verbalizes their families' concerns and point out that they face serious conflicts with their families as a result of working and living in Dahab. Sameh, a 25-year-old man from Cairo, shows how the migration of young men to Dahab causes great anxiety within their families:

> *My father does not talk to me anymore. He thinks that Dahab is an evil place. He does not even talk to me when I call to ask about them. It causes me a lot of pain when I phone my family and I know that he is sitting next to my mother, but refuses to talk to me.*

Mahmoud has the same dilemma with his family:

> *In spite of the fact that I support my family with some money whenever possible, they are not convinced that I should stay and work in this place. They believe that I should go back to finish my education and look for a decent job.*

Moreover, the fact that men form casual relationships with foreign women is worrisome to their families and at times they consider forcing them to leave Dahab and return to their homes. Hany explains that a father of one of his friends traveled to Dahab and compelled him to leave. He also added that his family is not content that he lives and works in Dahab, he says:

> *When my uncle heard that I got married to a tourist here, he called me and threatened that he come to take me back with him if I did not*

> *stop this behavior. My mother also worries a lot about me. Whenever I call her, she always tells me about her worries. She always prays and says: 'May God keep bad women and men out of your way'* (Rabena yeb'id 'anak banat wa awlad al-haram). *I always laugh when she says that and tell myself: 'Please mother say: 'Bad men only'* (awlad al-haram bas).

On one hand, young men are aware that their families are concerned about them and that the conflicts between them and members of their families stem from the mere fact that they want the best for them. On the other, the young men believe that their parents are traditional in the way they think and that they want to impose certain regulations on them which are inappropriate for today's life-style. Thus, conflicts arise between them and their families.

The Society, State Control, and Regulations

Interestingly, my informants explain that they do not have any conflicts with the society. In contrast, many of them mention that their friends are envious of them for having a job and for being able to establish relationships with foreign women. However, they also explain that men in Dahab are stigmatized since it is widely known that sexual freedom and drug abuse are common phenomena there.

Furthermore, the majority of the informants complain of the way the police treats them simply because they are Egyptians. They explain that in Dahab the police exercises power over Egyptians only and, at times, deports them for no obvious reason. At the same time, it does not interfere when foreigners work in the tourist businesses without work permits. They further add that the police tries to regulate relationships between Egyptian men and foreign women but does not have any form of control over relationships that take place between foreign men and women. Kamel, a 25-year-old man from Mansoura has been working in Dahab for six years. Commenting on the double standards of the police, he says:

> *On one hand, policemen chase Egyptian men who try to establish relationships with foreign women. On the other, they leave foreigners to commit indecent acts in the center of the town and do not say anything. They interfere only once an Egyptian is involved even if he were only walking with a woman on the beach.*

On several occasions, my informants told me that the police checks on them even in their houses to see if they live with foreign women outside of wedlock.

Foucault in his book *History of Sexuality* describes how sex became a police matter and traces the history of this issue to the beginning of the eighteenth century:

> [S]ex was not something that one simply judged; it was a thing one administered. It was in a nature of public potential; it called for management procedure; it had to be taken charge of by analytical discourses. In the eighteenth century, sex became a 'police' matter in the full and strict sense given the term at the time. (1979:24)

He explains that new sexual norms appeared during this period.

> Through pedagogy, medicine and economics, it made sex not only a secular concern, but a concern of the state as well .... Sex became a matter that required the social body as a whole, and virtually all of its individuals to place themselves under surveillance. (Foucault 1979:116)

However, he further argues that the "policing of sex" was "not the rigor of a taboo, but the necessity of regulating sex through useful and public discourses" (Foucault, 1979:25).

The policing of sex in Dahab is "to protect the traditions of the society," as argued by the lawyer. When asked about the actions of the police and the factthat there is no law in Egypt that regulates relationships between foreigners and Egyptians or any type of relationships outside of marriage, he answered: "The police does not need a law to act in this manner."

The informants' explanations of why the police authorities behave in this manner show an egocentric approach to the world where others' actions are interpreted in relation to oneself. According to Girgis:

> Policemen are jealous because they cannot do what we do. Therefore, they try to bother us when they see any of us with a foreign woman. I am sure they would do the same if they had the chance. The other day, a policeman came with a foreign woman and stayed with her in one of the hotels. They stayed in two different rooms, but the intentions were clear.

Sayed, a 26-year-old man from Behira also projected his own point of view saying: "The fact that we can speak foreign languages and the policemen cannot does not make them very happy. Therefore, they exercise their power to show that they are better than we are."

However, I understand that the actions of the police in Dahab and their strict interference to keep Egyptian men and foreign women apart originate from the fact that the authorities do not want any conflicts to happen between Egyptians and tourists. When conflicts arise policemen have to work and have to investigate the issue. However, when Egyptian men and foreign women do not interact with each other, there would be no conflicts. In the case of marriage, any disagreement becomes a "family affair," which the police does not have to handle. Sue, a 34-year-old British woman who has been living in Dahab for two years and married in a *'urfi* manner to an Egyptian man, told me the following incident that affirms this opinion:

> Our house was robbed; somebody broke in and stole lots of our belongings. When we reported the robbery to the police, they did not take any action. They told me, 'We cannot do anything about it, it is your husband who stole your stuff,' and they did not believe me when I told them that his money was also stolen.

If the thief was the husband then the case would be filed under "family affair" and the police would not have to do anything about it. However, in spite of the grievances verbalized by many of the informants, they believe that the police authorities in Dahab are not as authoritarian as in other parts of Egypt and explain that the possibility to meet foreigners and establish relationships with them is easier in Dahab than in any other place in Egypt. The reiterate that the only way to resolve the conflicts between them and the police is to get a *'urfi* marriage contract.

Religion

Respect for religion is part of the cultural heritage of the Egyptian society. Even when the actions of people contradict the teachings of religion they still show high level of appreciation and respect of religious norms.

Despite the fact that none of the young men I interviewed showed any interest in practicing religion in their daily life, all of them pronounced their respect to religion and their understanding that their conduct in Dahab cannot be justified by it. Some of them even have shown regret that they have adopted behaviors that contradict the teachings of religion. Others have expressed the feeling that their attitude toward religion and God has experienced a shift since the time they have migrated to Dahab. As Hany puts it clearly:

> *I used to pray regularly before I came to Dahab. My attitude towards God was very strong and very spiritual. Now, my relationship is very strange. I always ask God to help me find a woman and when I have a partner, I ask him to protect me from the police.*

Similar to other cultural aspects of their life, young men in Dahab are alienated from the main culture in respect of their religious practices. Furthermore, in many cases they adjust religion to fulfill their needs.

Availability of Drugs

Few would dispute that access to illegal drugs is one of the primary factors that attract young Egyptian men and tourists to Dahab. This access is one of the reasons why Dahab has the reputation of being like Amsterdam. I have observed Egyptian men smoking *hashish* with female tourists in the cafes along the sea. According to my informants, in the past couples occasionally engaged in sex on the beach after using drugs. However, the extensive presence of the police has limited dealing with drugs during the past few years, especially after a sharp crackdown on drug dealers in 1998. In spite of this fact, obtaining drugs seems to be relatively easy in Dahab or in other parts nearby. However, a more detailed investigation into recreational drug use is needed to acquire further information about the kinds of drugs used and the social background of drug users.

Conclusion

Over the past few decades, the economic adversity in the Egyptian society has affected large segments of the population at the grass-root level who subsequently resorted to different ways to generate incomes to survive the socio-economic problems in the society. Moreover, marriage has become unaffordable to many young people and the age of marriage has risen which eventually led to the appearance of the *'urfi* marriage phenomenon as a response to these difficulties.

Although it is easy for young Egyptian men working in Dahab to interact with foreign female tourists and establish relationships with them, the extensive presence of the police is an obstacle for them to interact freely with foreign women. Consequently, they capitalize on *'urfi* marriage in order to find solutions to the strict rules imposed by the police. *'Urfi* marriage is the young men's tool to legitimize the sexual relations they have with foreign tourists. This, however, jeopardizes their relationships with their families, religion, society, and societal norms.

Chapter 5
Constructing Sexuality, Sexual Health, and Risk
Male and Female Discourses in Dahab

HUMANS ARE SOCIAL beings; their experiences in life are structured within social relationships. Social interactions take place in different forms depending on the level of closeness and the surrounding circumstances. Sexuality is considered one of the most intimate levels of possible relations among humans and is known to have a direct impact on the general well-being of a person.

According to the WHO (1975) as cited in Collumbien and Hawkes (2000), sexual health is defined as "the integration of somatic, emotional, intellectual and social aspects of sexual being" (Collumbien and Hawkes, 2000:135). Our attitudes toward sex and sexuality affect our life as well as our perceptions of other people. Further, the conceptions of sex and sexuality differ according to the culture and the ideologies adopted in a given society. In some cultures pre-marital sex is acceptable, while in others sexuality is not permitted to be practiced outside of wedlock. This can be observed in Muslim societies where sexual intercourse is not acceptable among couples unless they are married.

In South Asian traditional societies, Dixon-Mueller (1996) argues that sexual activity before the age of marriage is not permissible and is socially acceptable only after a certain age. She gives another example of contrasting practices among the Kung in Botswana, and explains that child sex play is acceptable in this society and sometimes even encouraged. Among this group, the age of sexual experimentation with several partners is the adolescence period, while early adulthood is the time of marriage. The period of menopause is considered to be a transitional stage for a more relaxed and free female sexuality in which a woman can take younger male partners.

The kind of relationship and the frequency of sexual expression are very important factors for sexual and reproductive health. In some types of sexual involvements there is no need to use contraceptives to prevent pregnancy, such as in the case of the elder women engaged in sexual relationships with younger men because there is no fear of pregnancy. However, the use of certain types of contraceptives among this group is highly important and recommended for the prevention of sexually transmitted diseases.

It is beyond doubt that health in general is affected by the behavior adopted by individuals. Sexual health in particular is extremely endangered by various types of sexually transmitted diseases (STDs). Acquired Immune Deficiency Syndrome (AIDS) is considered to be the most dangerous epidemic that has inflicted humanity since the emergence of the first AIDS case in the early 1980s.

Since the discovery of AIDS, people's perception of sexuality has changed dramatically and the human expression of sexual needs has taken a different scope. The risk of contracting STDs has become one of the factors involved in sexuality and sexual behavior. Negotiating sexuality has become an important facet for many people in order to avoid risks and health hazards. Condoms have been introduced not only as contraceptives but also as a preventive method against diseases. However, risk is a human construct, and the perception of risk differs from one person to another. According to Johnson and Covello (1987), risk is subjective and linked to a specific situation and anyone's perceptions "are no more valid than the perceptions of any other" (Johnson and Covello, 1987:3). Some think of risk only when fearing that their life, health, or wellbeing is endangered, whereas others feel that they are at risk all the time.

The focus of this chapter is sexuality, reproductive health, and risk among the group of Egyptian men and foreign women in Dahab. I attempt to reveal how the young men and foreign women construct their understanding around their own sexuality, health and the risks closely linked to their behavior. I also examine how the social circumstances surrounding the young men in Dahab have affected their perceptions of their own 'selves' and the 'Other.'

Constructions of Sexuality

It is difficult to talk about sexuality, markedly so in the Egyptian society where sexuality is a taboo subject. However, the men in Dahab talk openly about their sexual activities. According to my observations, the conversations between them are centered on women and sex. The comments that foreign women hear in the streets, addressed to them in English or Arabic, are highly sexual. Similar to the Palestinian men described by Bowman (1989), the men in Dahab regard foreign women as an opportunity to have an outlet for their sexual frustration, social degradation, and submission to the police authorities. In spite of the fact that they describe foreign females as women who are "lacking something", they still consider them as desirable sexual objects and a venue for marriage and migration. As Jane, a 31-year-old British woman[10] explains:

> *Dahab is less aggressive in terms of selling than everywhere else in Egypt, such as Cairo and Luxor, where they try to sell you stuff rather than approaching a female to have sex. Everywhere else they want your money, while here they want you rather than your money.... While sitting in one of these camps you listen to one of the Egyptians bragging about how he pulled this girl from England and having a different woman every night and talking about which girl he has tonight.*

As mentioned earlier, Blumer (1969) explains that the action of the people toward objects is based on the meanings they carry for them. When I asked my informants which meaning sex carries for them, I got the following answers. Said, a 25-year-old man from Cairo, who has been living in Dahab for five years and works in a cafeteria, says: "Sex is like sports; it is fun, relaxation; it is just a feeling." For Samy, a 24-year-old man from Mansoura, who works as a shopkeeper, and has been living in Dahab for four years without involving himself in any sexual relations with foreign women due to the language barrier, points out: "For me it means that I sleep with any woman." George, a 23-year-old man from Sohag who works in a camp and has been living in Dahab for two and a half years, declares: "For me it means enjoyment. I came to Dahab especially for this purpose." Omar, a 22-year-old man from Luxor, who works in a shop and has been living in Dahab for nine years, also shares George's opinion and believes the meaning sex conveys for him is "enjoyment."

One can observe that sexuality for the men in Dahab connotes momentary pleasure that does not necessarily involve emotional attachment or social

---

10 Jane was interviewed after one week of her visit to Dahab. Although, she had been involved in a relationship with an Egyptian man, she had not yet been able to gain insights into the dynamics of relationships motivated by economic benefits.

responsibility to the women within the relationship. As mentioned earlier, their construction of sexuality stems from a fulfillment of their needs and desires regardless of feelings and the personality of the woman involved, who sometimes can be thirty years older than they are, as long as she helps them to reach their final goal, which is to travel abroad. One can easily see that the constructed meaning of sexuality varies considerably from what most Egyptians believe about sex and sexual relationships. The common opinion is that sex has to take place within marriage to build a family and to have children.

Constructions of Health

In general, people tend not to talk about their health when they are healthy. They talk about it only when they feel that it is endangered or being affected by something. However, my interviews in Dahab reveal that the young people are aware of the hazards that can arise due to their sexual behavior. They live with a constant sense of insecurity about their health, though they do not take any prophylactic steps to protect themselves. Moreover, they believe in different ways of protection. For instance, they consider returning to religion and staying away from women as the best means to protect themselves against disease.

However, few of the young men I spoke with have not shown any intention to stop their behavior. Others showed fear of diseases; yet, this fear has not materialized to affect their behavior. Mohamed[11] explains: "Diseases worry me a lot, especially after I read about AIDS in the newspaper. Therefore, I decided to keep away from foreign women." Medhat, a 24-year-old man from Sohag, who works in a camp and has been living in Dahab since 1995, articulates his concerns about his health:

> Very often I think about my health. A friend of mine got a contract to work abroad and he had to get some medical tests done as a prerequisite to get the job. At this moment I started to think about AIDS and the other diseases. It worried me so much that every now and then I think about it and wonder if I have these diseases. AIDS is the disease that concerns me most, because it does not appear immediately on the carrier compared to other diseases.

---

11 I saw Mohamed trying to approach a Japanese tourist before the interview, who also waited for him until we finished the interview and they went off together.

George also verbalizes his worries about his health:

> I always think about my health. Diseases are the most dangerous hazards that could affect our health. You know... foreign women as well as Egyptian women could transmit diseases to you, but foreign women know how to avoid diseases, they always ask me to use a condom, while Egyptian women do not even know what a condom is. Egyptian women might be menstruating and do not tell you in contrast to foreign women who ask me to use a condom and I can tell if they have their period or not.

It is clear that George has a stereotypical view of Egyptian women as being uneducated concerning sexuality and health issues in contrast to foreign women who try to protect themselves and their partners from any undesired consequences.

Nader, a 24-year-old man from Cairo, a literature student who works in Dahab as a waiter in a cafeteria, always thinks about his health and worries about any illness that could affect the function of his organs:

> Of course I think about my health. In fact, foreign women think about health more than I do because they have extensive health awareness. I think about the condom before anything because of two main reasons: Firstly to protect my health and secondly to secure the woman's approval who would not accept to have sex with me without it. However, I prefer to have intercourse without it because it feels much better, but I always fear prostitutes and the madlu'een.[12]

Nader's expression of his worries about his health when prostitutes and women who directly ask for sex or show any sexual desires are involved illustrates how men in Dahab construct their ideas about their health as well as about the women. A woman whom they approach can be a potential sex partner and is perceived as being of no risk for them; however, the same woman would be considered a source of danger if she shows interest in having sex.

Mohamed also agrees with Nader by making the following statement: "When a woman comes here and shows sexual desires, we know immediately that she has AIDS; therefore, we avoid her."

---

12 *Madlu'een* is a slang word that, in this context, means the ones who show a strong desire of having sex.

Chapter 5: Constructing Sexuality, Sexual Health, and Risk

Perceptions of Risk

Most of the informants have shown some knowledge about STDs, especially AIDS. Risk is mainly constructed on the grounds of the knowledge they have about STDs and AIDS. Their consciousness of risk also translates into their choice of partners or potential sex partners who are evaluated according to their appearance, cleanliness, as well as their behavior. A woman who appears not to be clean is considered a potential risk.

Johnson and Covello explain that, "[r]isk is only what people say it is" (1987:3). As mentioned earlier, for most of the men in Dahab, a woman who shows sexual desire or is very flirtatious is considered to be a potential source of risk as Mohamed explains:

> *It happened that a foreign woman came to Dahab and tried to make contacts with men, but we knew that she was a carrier of a disease because of her behavior and warned each other. She wanted to have sex with anyone, even if she would have to pay money. She went from one shop to the other flirting with men. At the end she was arrested by the police.*

When I asked Mohamed about the meaning of risk to him, his answer shows how some men in Dahab do not take the relationships they establish with foreign women seriously and illustrates that often when they think about marriage and establishing a family they go back to their cultural roots and marry an Egyptian woman, which adds another dimension to the health implications. He says:

> *It is risky when I sleep with an infected woman since in this case the AIDS virus can be transmitted to me; and when I get married to an Egyptian woman it can also be transmitted to her and consequently to the children.*

This proved to be a genuine concern since in some cases men indeed sought Egyptian wives when they decided to establish a family and have children.

Hamdy, a 23-year-old man from Alexandria, who works as a diving instructor and has been living in Dahab for three years, articulates his understanding of risk in a way similar to that of Mohamed:

> *Sometimes you find a woman coming to ask me to try things out with her under the water, e.g., a French kiss. Once we are out of the water she follows me everywhere attempting to have sex with me. I consider*

this woman to be of high potential risk. However, I can identify sick women from their appearance, the way they approach me, and also from their skin.

For Ahmed, a 25-year-old man from Giza who has been living in Dahab for a year and a half, the only risk that one encounters when having intercourse with a tourist is to contract diseases. He says: "In general there is no risk, but the only problem is diseases like AIDS. These can only be transmitted through sexual intercourse or blood transfusion, but there is no problem about touching or kissing." Samy has a similar point of view: "Diseases are the big risk; they can be transmitted through intercourse or blood. You know, the blood of the partners mixes up during intercourse, and this way one may catch the disease."

According to Maher, a 32-year-old man from Assiut who has been living in Dahab for four years, "Risk is exhibited when an organ of the body does not function. Encountering AIDS can be very risky because it destroys the immunity system of the body. It, among other dangerous diseases, spreads among foreign women who change men very frequently." For Medhat, risk has a similar meaning: "Diseases are the risk; not using a condom is equally risky." For Said, there is no threat against health; the only risk he could think of is to be a "lost person" *(daie')*, he adds:

> *I do not consider foreign girls to represent any kind of health risk to me. The nature here makes us relax and you need to be close to someone when you are relaxed [....] I know what I am doing. I do not go and sleep with anyone.... I use my senses in deciding if a woman carries any risk for me or not.*

This line of argument further shows that the men in Dahab rely on their intuition in determining whether or not a woman they meet is a carrier of a disease. Accordingly, they decide on establishing relationships with certain women, and refrain from others whom they conceive as sick or posing a potential risk for them.

Susan is a 26-year-old Australian tourist who spent a month in Dahab and established a relationship with an Egyptian man. She explains that she tried to avoid any risk at the beginning of her relationship. However, she found it difficult to insist on safe sex, arguing:

> *Any touching of the genitals even before the intercourse is very dangerous. The disease is the risk. But we tend to just ignore it. Egyptians*

Chapter 5: Constructing Sexuality, Sexual Health, and Risk 57

> *do not seem to worry about risk and, like many people all over the world, they think it won't happen to them. I was mad at him [her Egyptian partner] at the beginning when he did not use a condom, but it is always difficult to talk about this issue at the beginning of a relationship.*

However, Susan's partner, in a separate interview setting, stated that he always uses a condom during intercourse with his foreign partners so as to show that he is aware of the health hazards and that he takes precautions to avoid them. However, in a later discussion he admitted that he does not like to use a condom while in a relationship with a foreign female. This statement shows that there is often a discrepancy between the knowledge that the men in Dahab have and their actual practices.

Margaret, a 50-year-old woman from Switzerland, has been living in Dahab for a year and a half. She was involved in *'urfi* marriage twice. She expresses her concerns about health risks among the men in Dahab, but also refers to the fact that men do not end up marrying a foreign woman after having multiple relationships with tourists. On the contrary, when they want to start a family they marry an Egyptian woman.

> *People here are at risk because of their sexual behavior. Egyptian men and foreign women in Dahab are together only because of sex and money. Not many of them stay together forever. Egyptian men always go back to Egyptian women. Therefore, Egyptian women are also at risk because of their husbands' sexual history of having frequent sexual relationships with foreign women.*

Margaret supports the previous argument stated by Mohamed and adds another dimension to the problem. In spite of the fact that Egyptian women are not involved in the practices that take place in Dahab, they are vulnerable to diseases and might be affected directly by their husbands' pre-marital relationships, which will consequently have an impact on their children in the future.

Though the men in Dahab practice unsafe sexual behaviors, the interviewed doctor in this research denies that the men can be in danger. He claims that, "Egyptian men are clean *nudaf*, i.e., free from diseases, and this is the main reason why foreign women prefer to come here and establish relationships with them." He further illustrates that there are no health awareness programs or campaigns that explain to men the health hazards that can arise out of their behavior.

As one can easily observe, men's knowledge about STDs does not translate into having a feeling that they are at risk given their sexual practices. Relying on their beliefs that they are safe since they use their senses in assessing and selecting whom to interact and have a relationship with and whom to avoid, makes them believe that they do not need to take any measures to avoid risks that could endanger their health.

Risk and Protection
The perceptions of foreign women among the men in Dahab vary from being dirty, smelly, to being carriers of diseases and epidemics. Therefore, many men show insecurity about their health due to different kinds of sexual relations they establish with foreign women.

On the other hand, protection is constructed among them according to their needs. In general, they believe that there are three levels of protection: legal, physical, and moral. As mentioned before, for legal protection, they resort to *'urfi* marriage which takes place in the presence of a lawyer.

Physical protection entails means such as the use of condoms in order to avoid contracting diseases. In spite of the fact that the young men are aware of the potential danger of getting infected with STDs, resorting to physical protection is common among them only because foreign women insist on it. Egyptian men believe that the condom in itself is never enough and they always discuss the issue of protection with each other. Nevertheless, the majority of them have shown lack of interest in using it either because they are careless, or because of the unavailability of condoms at the time when they need them. According to Shady, a 27-year-old shopkeeper who is originally from Giza:

> *It could happen in the shop at a moment when I have no condoms. If I can convince a woman to have intercourse with her, I close the shop and after half an hour I open it again. I cannot run around and look for a condom. We do not think about it in such moments.*

Furthermore, men believe that any diseases can be transmitted even while using a condom, since "condoms also break." Therefore, they consider that they are still vulnerable even if they use it. Moreover, some of the foreign women have shown a different level of precaution by not having intercourse with anybody who does not use a condom. In addition, some of them ask their partners to have an HIV test once they take the decision to get married—a request that men have to fulfill—because, according to the women, the likelihood of having intercourse without using condoms is higher once they are married since they want to feel more relaxed with their husbands.

Finally, for most of the people in Dahab, the best protection is the moral one. They give credence to following the religion and the values of their society which they believe are the best means for protecting oneself against any hazard. However, if one is weak-willed and cannot stay away from women, then he relies on the two other levels of protection.

While, all of the Egyptian men and foreign women whom I interviewed consider AIDS to be the highest risk they could encounter from their behavior, most of my informants did not show any knowledge about other STDs besides AIDS. Only one foreign woman mentioned her worries about Hepatitis B and C, and one Egyptian man mentioned Syphilis. However, he did not show any concern about this disease since, according to him, "it is not as dangerous as AIDS."

The Relationship between Health and Sexual Satisfaction

Undoubtedly, the behavior people follow to express their sexual desires affects their health. However, some of the Egyptian informants claim that there is no relationship between sex, sexual behavior, and health. In addition, some of them express concerns about the lack of sexual satisfaction. They believe that having no access to sex might entail negative implications on their mental health since it could cause "frustration." They also explain that some men working in Dahab are unable to engage in sexual relationships with foreign women because of their limited language skills. Consequently, some of them approached women in a forceful manner to satisfy their sexual desires.

Some men adopt inappropriate behavior as they happen to live in an atmosphere where sexual practices abound while they are not able to compete with their peers in enjoying the atmosphere of sexuality. The story of Sara is a good example that illustrates this issue. Sara is an Australian young woman in her twenties. She describes how someone almost attacked her in the room where she was staying in a camp:

> *It was a hot day when I was lying in my bed with minimum clothes on and having the window of my room open. Suddenly, I open my eyes to find a man in the room standing next to my bed staring at me. I screamed and the people came to help me and luckily nothing happened.*

Moreover, some of the men think that there are women who come to Dahab to spread sexual diseases. However, only one of my informants told me that he knew a man who lost his potency due to a sexual disease that he contracted through intercourse with a foreign woman: "The disease made him impotent." On the other hand, a foreign woman, who was married to an Egyptian, got a vaginal infection and claimed she caught it from her husband.

The doctor and the pharmacists could not provide any information on STDs in Dahab claiming that whenever someone is infected they seek medical services in Cairo so as to guarantee anonymity. Besides, men go to Cairo to pursue any medical tests required by their foreign women.

The Main Actors
Throughout the conversations I had with Egyptian men and foreign women in Dahab, I understood that women come to Dahab to enjoy the nature and the sea. Men approach them with the intention to establish a relationship. In this regard women are the passive actors, because they do not initiate the relationships. According to Margaret:

> *No woman comes here to find men. It happens all over the world. I can go and do whatever I want in any other country, but I hate doing it here. Men here seek educated women to sleep with and want their local women to do everything else for them.*

Stretching the issue further, Jane says:

> *When you travel on your own and you are a female, you feel lonely sometimes. In this situation, when someone gives you attention, you might fall for him. I guess emotionally it has been very tough on some women who came here.*

Hence, one can see that men are the main actors in initiating relationships. However, the roles change once a relationship is established, since women take the main role by determining how to continue the relationship e.g. casual, long term, 'urfi or legalized marriage. This approach contrasts marriage and relationship patterns in the Egyptian society where men normally have the final say and determine the terms of the relationship.

Furthermore, while many women agree on having 'urfi marriages, many others refuse this kind of relationship because they do not want to commit themselves for any kind of marriage. In addition, foreign women are also the ones who decide about the enforcement of safe sex. According to the doctor, "Women force the men to use condoms." The fact that some women insist on the use of condoms makes some men consider carrying them along, since they know they cannot have access to women without them. In this regard, men play the passive role. In fact, my informants mentioned that most of the women come to Dahab and bring condoms with them. The pharmacists I interviewed in Dahab stressed the fact that foreign women are the main purchasers of condoms, whereas pills and other contraceptives prescribed by doctors, e.g. intrauterine devices (IUDs), are mostly used by Bedouin women. In some cases, according to some informants, women even bring medications for men to use in order to enhance pleasure during intercourse. Therefore, one can conclude that once the relationship is established women play an active role in shaping the relationship.

The Stereotypical Views of Egyptian Women versus Foreign Tourists

The interviews revealed that the informants have constructed stereotypical views of Egyptian women. Men in Dahab believe that Egyptian women do not ask for foreplay because they are hot-blooded *(damuhum sukhr)* and therefore, they do not need an extended period of sexual intercourse to achieve satisfaction. In contrast, foreign women are described as cold-blooded *(damuhum barid)* due to their articulation of their sexual needs. Accordingly, foreign women require longer intercourse to achieve satisfaction, which has to be preceded by an excessive foreplay. My interviewees describe how the foreplay with these women may last for hours, while only a touch can arouse Egyptian women who could be satisfied with five minutes of intercourse because they are always "ready" *(gahzeen)*.

This shows how Egyptian men are not aware of women's desires and confuse the expression of sexual needs with "coldness." Since Egyptian women do not express their sexual needs, men conceive them as "hot-blooded." Essam, a 35-year-old man from Beheira, who has been living in Dahab for fifteen years and established various relationships with foreign women, explains that Egyptian women do not need the kind of sexual relations demanded by foreign women. Now married to an Egyptian woman from whom he has two children, he expresses his frustration with his current relationship, saying: "Once you watch a video you can never go back and listen to the radio." When I showed that I did not understand his statement and solicited more clarification he said:

You cannot compare Egyptian women (radio) with foreign ones (video). There is a big difference. Egyptian women do not express their sexuality; they do not need long sexual intercourse. Maybe it is because of circumcision. While foreign women require longer time and ask even for more.

Essam's description shows how some men in Dahab view Egyptian women as traditional (radio) given the fact that they do not express their needs and do not show their sexual desires compared to the modern foreign women (video) who do not only articulate their needs, but also ask for more than what the Egyptian men normally would expect from a woman and explicitly communicate what they want in order to reach satisfaction. When I asked him if he tried to give his wife the same level of satisfaction that he used to give to foreign women and if he discussed this issue with her, he said: "No, because she does not need it, she never asks for it."

Mohamed also supports Essam's argument that Egyptian women do not require long sexual intercourse:

> *Intercourse with a foreigner differs from the one with an Egyptian. An Egyptian woman needs only five minutes, while foreign women need longer time to the level that one might get to the point of ejaculating blood,*[13] *which might make him weak and affect his sexual performance one day. Foreign women have cold blood* (damuhum barid); *therefore, they need more frequent sexual intercourses to reach satisfaction. Furthermore, they are not circumcised and this explains their need for a long intercourse, in contrast to Egyptian women who need a maximum of a minute or two for satisfaction.*

Mohamed's views of foreign women as cold-blooded who require a longer intercourse until the man "ejaculates blood" shows how the fear of women's sexuality is embedded in the culture and the background of the men in Dahab, which is comparable to the discourses of the men in San Blas in Spain studied by Brandes (1981) who believe that women's sexuality could endanger men's virility. Martin, examining the works of the nineteenth century writers and their fantasy of women, explains:

> *A woman would ruin a man, by her extravagant spending, by her demands on him to spend, or, in another realm, by her excessive*

---

13 There is a common belief among Egyptian men that an intercourse lasting a long time might lead to ejaculating blood, which would endanger man's health.

*demands on him for sex. Losing too much sperm meant losing that
which sperm was believed to manufacture. (Martin, 1992:34)*

This opinion is based on men's fear of females' sexuality and their excessive sexual needs. Women are also viewed to be the consumers of men and their semen.

From this we can see that the views held by Egyptian men about Egyptian women and foreign tourists are contradictory. On the one hand, foreign women are considered "cold-blooded" since they ask for foreplay and a long period of intercourse, but at the same time they are viewed as oversexed because they are not circumcised. On the other hand, the mere fact that most Egyptian women do not ask for the type of sexual relationships demanded by foreign women results in considering them to be "hot-blooded." Their "hot blood," according to my informants, is based on the fact that they are circumcised, which reduces their need for intercourse to "a minute or two." However, the common belief and justification to the practice of female circumcision is to limit women's sexuality (Dorkenoo, 1994). As a result, one can see that the men contradict themselves since they believe that Egyptian women are [hot-blooded] due to circumcision, a practice that is mainly used to reduce women's sexual desires and pleasures. Taking the male discourses in Dahab into consideration, one can argue that Egyptian women should be the ones who need a long period of intercourse and foreplay for satisfaction since their sexual desires are limited and reduced by circumcision.

This further illustrates how men in Dahab have traditional stereotypical views of Egyptian women and exercise their masculinity over them by false perceptions. Moreover, it also reveals that the notion of masculinity takes a different level when dealing with foreign women.

Agency and Desire: Who Is the Proactive Partner?

According to Foxhall, other than attraction, sexuality entails control, power and obedience (Foxall 1998, as quoted in Wassif and Mansour, 1999). In his book, *The History of Sexuality*, Foucault also argues that the sexual ideologies of Greek men involved a lot of domination, sovereignty and individuality:

> Greek male ideologies of sexuality have a lot to do with notions of control, autonomy and individuality. A very important source of man's power and authority as heads of households was that (ideally, at least) they could control the sexual activities of other household members

(including animals and slaves), but that they themselves were autonomous and no one else could dictate their sexual activities. But reality, however hard to get at, is usually more complicated than ideology. And this ideology works only as long as women are assumed to be passive and boys obedient. (Quoted in Wassif and Mansour, 1999:66)

The sexual dynamics in the Egyptian society are very similar to the Greek male ideologies that Foucault illustrates above. Sexuality in the Egyptian society always involves a power relation between men and women. In most of the cases, men are the ones who are supposed to initiate sex and have desires, while women should not have desires and should not show them.

In contrast, the discourses around sexuality in Dahab show that these dynamics work differently where foreign women, according to the informants, determine their needs and have power over their own sexuality and also that of their partners. While, they may not initiate a relationship with the Egyptian men when they arrive to Dahab, once a relation is established, they have the right not only to initiate sex but also to determine how the sexual activity should be carried out. Moreover, the agency of the foreign women entails that Egyptian men satisfy their sexual desires to a degree that does not match their behavior towards Egyptian women. What is more, foreign women decide the length of the relationship and the type of relation they want to have with the Egyptian men. In view of these discourses, I argue that in a largely male dominated society like Egypt, men in Dahab tend to play out their masculinity differently with foreign women and try to satisfy their emotional as well as physical needs in a manner that contrasts the situation with Egyptian women. In the latter case, women are subjugated by men who are the ones who put the terms of the relationship and possess an absolute right to divorce the wife, except for the case in which women solicit a *khul'* in court.[14]

Perceptions of the "Other" and the "Self"

The interactions that Egyptian men have with foreigners on a daily basis in Dahab have not only affected their sexual behaviors and masculinity but also their perceptions of themselves, the Other, and their own culture. In a society where by large sex is not freely debated, the men in Dahab create a unique culture for themselves away from control mechanisms, such as family,

---

14 *Khul'* is the right given to women to divorce themselves from their husbands in court. This has only been granted to them recently.

traditions, and the hegemonic culture of society. However, in a society based on gender biases, women are considered to be sexual objects rather than partners. The ways men approach women in Dahab and harass them are embedded in the culture they grew up in.

One can draw similarities between male practices in Dahab and the Glendiot men in Crete described by Herzfeld (1985). Similar to raiding in Crete, the men in Dahab approach women and persuade them to establish sexual relationships. Aggressive behavior, such as stealing sheep in order to make friends, and pursuing sexual relationships with women are used by men in both societies to magnify and assure their masculinity.

Many men in Dahab articulate their belief that foreign women are dirty and impure. Some of them think that foreign women commit disgusting acts, e.g. "oral sex," which is foreign to most of the Egyptians. They also explain that foreign women are unclean because they do not remove their bodily hair. Furthermore, they describe foreign women as impure due to the fact that they do not purify their bodies by ritual washings after menstruation or after having sex with them.

However, these same respondents show great admiration of the West and it believe it has the solution for their economic problems. They borrow superficial western customs, such as long hair and dreadlocks, thinking that such practices would attract western women to them. In this sense, they are torn between their own culture that they are estranged from, and the western culture that they cannot reach and which is only a fancy in their minds. The case is as Bayat puts it: "Living on the margin of two cultures without being a full member of either" (Bayat, 2000:536).

Globalization: Are we Heading There?
Waters (1995) argues that:

> *In a globalized world there will be a single society and culture occupying the planet. This society and culture will probably not be harmoniously integrated although it might conceivably be... no tight set of cultural preferences and prescriptions. Insofar as culture is unified it will be extremely abstract, expressing tolerance for diversity and individual choice. (Waters, 1995:3)*

In the Egyptian society, globalization manifests itself in different ways such as travel, tourism, and global patterns of material consumption. Within this context, new ideas about gender relations and sexuality are infiltrating the

Egyptian society, putting strains on more "traditional" notions of male–female relationships. As much as such processes create new opportunities for rethinking gender and sexual relations in Egypt, they are also a venue for western ideas about sexual relations and sex to penetrate the norms of Egyptian sexual practices.

Waters' view of a globalized culture and society can be verified in Dahab. There is a dominant culture that can also be found in many other parts of the world. It is a culture that gives space for difference and freedom of choice for each individual. In addition, this culture tolerates the variations of ideologies that people adopt and also puts people close together in spite of differences in religion, race, and social background. One can see that globalization has affected humans in many parts of the world not only socially and economically, but also with respect to intimate matters where common practices in the West were assumed to be the solution to the problems of many people around the world.

Some of the informants claim that what happens in Dahab will become a common culture. They justify this assumption by giving examples, such as the spread of *'urfi* marriage among young people in the Egyptian universities. They also state that in big cities, like Cairo, young men establish sexual relationships with Egyptian girls. However, this issue still needs to be investigated and verified.

Chapter 6
Femininity and Desirability
Foreign Female Discourses in Dahab

SIMILAR TO OTHER parts of the world, many tourist destinations in Egypt are promoted for their uniqueness and cultural specificity. Tourist industries construct these places as "unique" in terms of binary oppositions such as exotic versus ordinary, primitive versus developed, and local versus foreign. Advertising agencies are key players in promoting among tourists both the geographical place or destination and the cultural experiences they might share with the local community of the particular tourist site.

Sinai is one of these places conceived as unique which has been marketed for its history, nature, and Bedouin culture. Over the past two decades and particularly the end of the Israeli occupation, it has become the center of attention of the Egyptian government which has promoted it as a tourist destination. However, as explained earlier, investors have not developed tourist sites in Sinai equally. While investors have privileged high-scale tourist destinations, such as Sharm al-Sheikh, they have neglected others, such as Dahab and Nuweiba'. Consequently, the neglected areas became a fertile land for informal tourist businesses dominated mainly by young entrepreneurs who are interested in establishing cheap and informal tourist businesses. Subsequently, these areas emerged as tourist destinations for individual travelers and backpackers who mainly seek cheap accommodation and affordable tourist services.

Due to the reputation of Dahab among foreign tourists as an exotic and authentic place, it has become attractive for many foreign female travelers. In this chapter, I will specifically explore the hypothesis that western women's travels to Dahab re-inscribes traditional notions of "femininity" and gender differences rather than ensuring male-female equality. This contrasts the previously stated argument that: "[T]ravel has become part of the gendering activity of women as they seek to expand their gender repertoires to incorporate practices traditionally reserved for men and thereby integrate the conventionally masculine with the feminine" (Pruitt and LaFont, 1995 as quoted in Philips, 2001:189). I will further problematize this hypothesis by exploring the ways in which the same females, while seeking hyper-masculine males, simultaneously emasculate Egyptian males through sexual and gender negotiations as well as their racial, political, and economic power and privilege. In this regard, on the one hand, these women seek feminized experiences with hyper-masculine "Oriental" men, while on the other, they tend to dictate the terms of the relationship.

I will first start by examining foreign female discourses on western masculinities versus Egyptian masculinities. Then, I will explore the discourses of women regarding constructions of beauty and desirability. Finally, I will investigate the historical background of the relationships between Egyptian men and foreign women in Dahab that highlights colonial histories between the East and the West.

Discourses on Western Masculinity

A key point in this section is the argument that the Egyptian male discourse portrays western women in Dahab as females who travel to this destination because, according to my informants, western men "lack masculinity". Thus, they are there to seek "hyper masculine men," since these women are perceived to be equal to men in their societies and therefore play both gender roles at the same time.

In spite of all the gains that women in the West have achieved over the past few decades, the majority of the foreign female informants show unease about their position and the way they are treated by men in their societies. Many of them argue that despite the fact that they are the targets of harassment by Egyptian men in Dahab, once they are married to an Egyptian, they feel protected and safe, unlike the case in their societies where their physical safety is not guaranteed due to the high crime rates in their countries. They further argue that the classical model of the feminist movement in the West, which advocates equality between men and women, has caused a great deal of confusion on both sides. According to them, the feminist movement did indeed manage to improve the position of women in terms of equal personal

Chapter 6 Femininity and Desirability

opportunities, work, and legal rights. However, as a result of this, men have become confused about their role in society and, in many cases, do not know which role model to adopt in their behavior with women. A common example given by the female informants is the one of a man and a woman meeting at a door. The question arising here is: should the man open the door for the lady and invite her to pass first? My informants maintained that western men are currently confused about how to act in such a situation. If a man behaves according to the old role model and opens the door for the woman, he may be looked upon as an old-fashioned person who is thinks that women may not be able to do that by themselves. If he does not open the door, he may not be considered a gentleman. Christine, a 32-year-old French woman, involved in a *'urfi* marriage with an Egyptian man, points out that:

> *Western Europe made a mistake during the 1970s when women and men became equal and alike. The mistake is that there has become no difference between men and women. Most men are afraid of strong women in Europe. And instead of enjoying the benefits of equality, it only caused a problem. Women are not strong as men [in a physical sense], but if one woman wants to do a man's job, then why not?*

This statement reflects the problematic issue of equality. It refers to the freedom of choice that is taken as an unquestionable right: "If a woman wants to do a man's job, then why not?" Confusion, as the foreign female informants argue, has rendered it difficult for both men and women to act "naturally," which implies the existence of only one 'right' way of behavior prescribed by nature. This understanding of behavior is similar to that of a reflex, which is always triggered in response to a certain stimulus. It does not take into account that behavior is learnt through socialization and that it is socially constructed. In addition, this confusion reflects on many aspects of social life in the West that have affected male-female interactions on different levels, especially with regard to intimate relationships. The informants claim that men in the West fear responsibilities and burdens, particularly those that involve marriage and the establishment of a family.

Moreover, western females in Dahab view western males as "closed," "unprotective," "careless," "cold" and "unable to express their feelings." These attributes can be summarized in the words of one of the informants explaining that men in the West "relate to women differently than the Egyptian men in Dahab do." This discourse is similar to the discourse of the female sex tourists that describes men in the Caribbean Islands as different from Western men (Davidson and Taylor, 1999).

Furthermore, the female informants in Dahab argue that people in the West lead a materialistic life-style and work like "machines" in order to gain money and buy luxury equipment. All these preoccupations do not give people the time to interact with each other, to meet and talk on the same level as in Dahab. Helga, 52-year-old German woman argues that, "Face-to-face interactions are disappearing in the West, women and men do not meet each other due to their busy schedules and the only way to get to know someone is through the Internet."

Given the position foreign women occupy in their own societies, one can observe that they reach a new level of emotional satisfaction in Dahab and experience their femininity differently, a feeling that they scarcely encounter when dealing with western men, as they explain. Moreover, they value the way that the Egyptian men in Dahab treat them, which is not influenced by western beliefs that entail equality between males and females.

Discourses on Egyptian Masculinity

Shohat and Stam (1994) give a historical background on how the Arab, Eastern men and women are constructed in the Western media. They show how in the West images of Arab, Eastern women and men are viewed as in "heat" versus Western women and men who are perceived as "frigid" (1994:157).

The foreign female informants view Egyptian men in Dahab as being different since these men have not been exposed to the western models of femininity and masculinity. The way they act and deal with women is not tainted with complications that have been created by the feminist movements of the West. Their constructions of these men vary from being "kind," "caring," "nice," "helpful," to being "friendly." Maria, a Dutch 50-year-old woman gives the following description of the men in Dahab: "People can go inside you here, they can read your face and have a language for emotions, and are not shy to show it."

Additionally, Egyptian men are described as "family men," "open," and "responsible." The informants show satisfaction with the fact that their Egyptian partners take care of tasks related to the household, e.g. construction, carpentry, plumbing, while they do not have to get involved in these issues as compared to their own Western societies where they have to deal with all these matters on their own.

In this regard, one can observe that Western women in Dahab seek an alternative form of masculine experiences with Egyptian men, in which the male acts as a "family man," a "caring" and a "protective" partner. Anna,

Chapter 6: Femininity and Desirability

a 34-year-old Swiss woman says: "Many women like to have a family with a responsible man." Simone, a 23-year-old French student who specializes in Arabic and Islamic studies, says that she traveled to Egypt to experience the Arab and Islamic culture and compare it to the way they study it in the West. She also shows her satisfaction and happiness with the way she is being treated by "Arab" men, arguing that the difference between them and western men is that Arab men treat the woman as a "child." Foreign females in Dahab appreciate the "over protecting" character of the Egyptian males as Britta, a Swedish 32-year-old woman comments: "Egyptian men do not like other men looking at their wives." Moreover, there is a common belief among the Western women in Dahab that Egyptian men are charming and know how to satisfy women emotionally and sexually and to make the "tourist happy."

The informants' discourses on Egyptian men show how the western model of feminism has failed for this group and has not satisfied their needs as women. Yvonne, a 31-year-old Danish, clearly showed how the feminist movement did not meet her emotional needs:

> *Being alike [men and women in the West] made romance slowly disappear and that is what attracts women to this place [Dahab], which they find fascinating because men are not afraid of being men and romantic; and women are not afraid of being women and weak. Men here are not afraid of being men by treating a woman like a woman. The men here force us to be feminine.... My relationship to men in the West is based on friendship and I cannot imagine being with a Western man. Everything in the West is defined in terms of friendship.*

In light of the discourses of the Western female informants, one can argue that their encounters in Dahab change their view of themselves. Their experiences in Dahab help them to view themselves as feminine women who are desirable and protected by "masculine" Egyptian men. Moreover, their critique of the feminist movement in the West does not only focus on the way it shapes their position as women in their societies but also on its impact on western men. In addition, one can also see that these women are attracted to Egyptian men. However, this attraction is constructed through 'exotification,' 'racialization' and 'Otherness', which are based on the perception of the men's charm and care. Interestingly, the local men's involvements with female tourists are based on these notions of 'difference' and 'otherness.' They both use their 'difference' as a means to attract each other.

Furthermore, it is obvious that the way the East is constructed in western academia and media plays an important role in shaping the way western women perceive the Egyptian men in Dahab by stressing their masculinity and gender differences. Finally, the accounts of women in Dahab are used to magnify their femininity by seeking experiences that affirm their desirability and attractiveness on one hand. However, the same women try hard to stabilize their control over the relationship and their partners while leading an autonomous lifestyle and enjoying the freedom and equality that the feminist movement, which they criticize, has granted them. Such accounts are similar to female sex tourists in the Caribbean who establish sexual relations with locals and:

> *Employ fantasies of Otherness not just to legitimate obtaining sexual access to the kind of young fit handsome bodies... and to obtain affirmation of their own sexual desirability... but also to obtain a sense of power and control over themselves and others as engendered sexual beings and to affirm their own privilege as Westerners. (Davidson and Taylor, 1999:49–50)*

Western Femininity as a Site of Power and Privilege

As argued previously, the Western female tourists in Dahab seek experiences that magnify their femininity in which they are protected and also flattered by their Egyptian male partners. However, they also exercise different means of control and power over the men with whom they are involved and the relationship established. In spite of their attraction to the locality (Dahab) and the masculine, caring and protecting Egyptian men, in many cases, female tourists are not willing to carry out a serious relationship with Egyptian men and limit their commitment to the geographical location of Dahab. A common practice among many of the couples who have *'urfi* marriages in Dahab is that the women live in their countries and frequent Dahab to pay a visit to their Egyptian partners during their holidays. Furthermore, they do not consider taking their Egyptian partners to their native countries to meet their families and friends. This shows that limiting the relationship to Dahab by having a casual relationship or even a *'urfi* marriage is used as means to exercise control over the relationship and also over their partners. Acting in this manner, the women involved in these relationships can terminate the relationship whenever they want. Moreover, they are aware that being officially married to an Egyptian gives their partners the possibility to

Chapter 6: Femininity and Desirability

obtain visas to travel to their countries. This would mean a limitation to their freedom and a loss of control over the relationship. As a result, in many cases, females limit the relationship to Dahab and decide the time of their visit and the duration of their stay.

Furthermore, to a certain extent, these relationships, in which the women tend to dictate their terms on their partners, emasculate the men who are brought up in a 'male dominated' society and socialized to be the decision makers of the family and to have full control over the relationship and over their partners. In their encounters with foreign women, the men in Dahab actually give up part of their power and control, which is also viewed as part of their masculinity. In this sense, there is a partial switch of gender roles in these relationships. It is worth reiterating that women also decide the way the sexual activity is carried out and sometimes impose certain practices considered foreign to the Egyptian men. They have the agency of making Egyptian men satisfy their sexual, physical and psychological needs in spite of the fact that the men perceive them as having some sort of deficiency because they do not meet their constructions of beauty.

While the men in Dahab try hard to fulfill the demands of their foreign partners, it is unthinkable or unacceptable for them to accommodate the Egyptian women's needs whom they view as 'hot-blooded' and not in need of what a 'cold-blooded' western woman requires. Here the males' submission to foreign women in Dahab their efforts to satisfy their desires do not stem from the fear of *fitna* or chaos as is commonly believed in society. Rather these are the means to boost their own masculinity and capitalize on the established relationship with the foreign tourists to overcome the economic difficulties and may be get a chance to leave for the West. On the other hand, men do not need to prove their masculinity with Egyptian women, since this is an image they already have and is taken for granted by the society.

The agency of Western females in Dahab is also obvious with regard to control over the children. When a foreign woman gets pregnant, the delivery of the baby usually takes place in her own country away from her partner. As a result, the child is named after the mother, who is considered a single mother. In this case, the father has no legal power over the child who is also not entitled to obtain the Egyptian citizenship. During the course of my fieldwork, I observed several cases in which men have no access to their children and may have not even seen them at all, given the fact that they cannot afford the travel-expenses and cannot obtain entrance visas to their partners' countries. Susanna is a 36-year-old Norwegian who is involved in a *'urfi* marriage with an Egyptian. During her unplanned pregnancy, she decided to travel to her country in order to give birth to her baby. Now she lives in Norway with her child and returns to Dahab only for short vacations as a tourist to see her husband. During these visits the father is unable to communicate with his son, who speaks only Norwegian. In spite of the fact that this couple has been married for several years, Susanna has neither shown willingness to legalize this marriage nor has taken any steps in arranging for her partner to visit her country to introduce him to her family and friends. She says: "I have a feeling that the people will look down on me in the West if I take my husband with me. Also, there is no job for him there."

The issue of the children who are the fruit of 'urfi marriages represents a major concern for many men in Dahab. Some of the women left Egypt during their pregnancy and have never returned with the children. Some of the men know that they have a child but have no access to their children and have no means to see them. One of the informants once expressed his sadness because he has a 4-year-old daughter in France whom he has never seen since the mother left upon her pregnancy and never returned. He explains that he cannot travel to see his daughter and the only possibility to contact his daughter and to ask about her well-being is to phone the mother whenever possible. This summarizes lots of men's stories in Dahab who in many cases have no access to their children and lack the means to see them.

When I asked the lawyer about the legal status of these children and the possibility of their obtaining the Egyptian citizenship according to the Egyptian law, he explained:

> *The fact that the 'urfi marriage is not desirable in the Egyptian society does not mean that the Egyptian law does not approve of granting the children of these marriages the Egyptian citizenship when they are born here. However, the issue is very complicated in the cases of children who are born abroad. Therefore, in many instances the fathers consider registering the children in Egypt upon the return of the kids with their mothers in order to issue them birth certificates. If they do not do that, there is no possibility for the child to obtain the Egyptian citizenship.*

This explains the legal problems arising from the 'urfi marriages in Dahab and it shows to what extent foreign women have more legal rights over the children compared to the Egyptian men. In this context the men have no rights over their children and, in some cases, are not even able to see them unless their partners grant them this right.

On the other hand, the majority of the female informants show unease to help their partners to go with them to their home countries expressing, their worries about the men experiencing a "cultural shock." Some also articulate their concerns about the availability of jobs in their countries for their partners. However, one can argue that the geographical and temporal limitations of the relationships are used as means of control that give the foreign women the possibility to travel and experience forms of interactions and interracial sex that they tend not to choose in their countries of origin. Moreover, restricting these interactions to the geographical locality of Dahab allows foreign women to maintain a respectable reputation in their communities of origin where relationships with men from the Third World might stigmatize, marginalize, and mark them as deviants from the model expected of them in their own societies as 'white women'. This behavior is also exhibited by female sex tourists to the Caribbean who establish sexual relationships with black males, but would not want to have an overt relationship with a black male in their countries. These women "can transgress the racialized and gendered codes that normally govern their behavior, while maintaining their honor and reputation back home" (Davidson and Taylor, 1999:50).

Desirability and Beauty

In this section, I will analyze the western females' discourses on desirability and beauty, building upon the particular discourse adopted by Egyptian men who are involved in informal sexual relations with foreign females in Dahab. According to this discourse, these tourists cannot find partners in their countries since they do not meet the constructed standards of beauty in their own societies. As a result, they seek physical as well as emotional satisfaction through establishing relationships with men in Dahab, so that they can magnify their sense of femininity by feeling desired.

During my fieldwork in Dahab I observed several cases of young men forming sexual relationships with middle-aged women. In many cases the age difference was twenty years or more. Contemplating the female discourses in Dahab shows how the economic power of the western females is deemed crucial in the formation of these relationships. These women argue that buying a house for a young man or helping him start a business can be a good incentive to urge him to start a relationship with an older woman. Moreover, they rationalize their involvement in relationships with young men by claiming that, generally speaking, access to men in the West has become difficult. The demographic profile in the West shows that women in general and older women in particular outnumber men and that the number of these women is rapidly increasing. This makes many middle-aged Western women attracted to young Egyptian men in Dahab. Sophia, a 55-year-old

Dutch woman married to a 30-year-old Egyptian, says: "The feeling of the Egyptian man as a young child playing makes him desirable." Others believe that middle-aged women are vulnerable in Dahab because they leave their countries to escape some familial crisis, such as a divorce. When they come to Dahab and are approached by young men, they fall very easily without taking into consideration that the young men are not interested in them but in their money and in using them as a means to migrate to the West.

Furthermore, many of the foreign female informants who are married to Egyptians and have been living in Dahab for some years try to justify the actions and the practices of Western females in Dahab using the same discourse as that of the Egyptian males, arguing that many women cannot find partners in the West since they are "ugly" or "fat." However, the same women who do not match the idealized Western beauty constructs and who are described as "ugly" or "fat" are the ones considered to be sexual objects in Dahab. They are chased, romanced and, in many cases, loved and married. It is easy for them to find partners in Dahab because, as some women argue, Egyptian men use these liaisons to be able to travel to the West. Therefore, men in Dahab are desperate to establish a relationship with any woman regardless of her age, physical appearance or background in order to be able to have access to the West.

Moreover, the female informants in Dahab clarify that the Egyptian men's strategies of dealing with women such as "sweet talk" and "sense of humor" are very important components to discover something new about themselves. The feeling they gain as desired women with feminine qualities that qualifies them to be flattered and romanced, helps them temporarily to forget about the differences between them and the men in Dahab. Katja, a German middle-aged woman in her fifties, married to a young Egyptian man in his twenties explained that "sex" helps people to get closer to each other and that "through sex and sexuality, differences disappear, exactly like people who share their food and eat together."

Interestingly, in many cases foreign women do not attribute the interest of young Egyptian men in Dahab to either certain material benefits or to physical attraction. Rather, they believe that the locality of Dahab gives them the opportunity to interact with men who, consequently, help them to discover their femininity. They also view the men in Dahab as masculine, hypersexual. and protective who know how to deal with women and make them "feel like women" regardless of the age differences, which disappear with sex. Similar to these accounts, Sanchez Taylor (2001) in her study on the Caribbean, explains that constructions of local men as being hypersexual who have no control over their sexuality are justifications used by white women to explain the young men's interest in having sex with old and, in many cases, overweight women, overlooking the fact that these men are attracted to them only for material gains.

Post-Colonialism and Modernity

For western colonial powers "the Orient" was an exotic place. It was the fancy that haunted the imagination of many western male travelers. In his book *The Colonial Harem*, Malek Alloula (1986) explains how Arab women were imagined by westerners and how western photographers and painters portrayed them as:

> *Arrayed in the brilliant colors of exoticism and exuding a full-blown yet uncertain sensuality, the Orient, where unfathomable mysteries dwell and cruel and barbaric scenes are staged, has fascinated and disturbed Europe for a long time. It has been its glittering imaginary but also its mirage. (Alloula, 1986:3)*

Therefore, the discovery of the mysteries of the Orient and the access to its women was the goal of many male travelers. Books such as the 'Arabian Nights' were sources to construct a picture of the Orient, the Muslim world, the women as well as the *harem*. For years, many Western male travelers fantasized about the women of the Orient, the veil and the *harem* and were fascinated by these ideas (Mabro, 1991). As Edward Said put it: "The Orient was a place where one could look for sexual experience unobtainable in Europe" (1978:190). These phantasms were developed during the time of colonial projects in order to satisfy desires that Westerners could not fulfill in their societies. This fact is explained by Stoler who argues that:

> *[C]olonial power relations can be accounted for and explained as a sublimated expression of repressed desires in the West, of desires that resurface in moralizing missions, myths of the 'wild woman,' in a romance with the rural 'primitive,' or in other more, violent, virile, substitute form. (Stoler, 1995:167–8)*

Nevertheless, it can be generally assumed that Western travelers were not able to meet women or observe them since women were confined to the private spheres. Private spheres, like the *harem*, were used to differentiate between men and women not only by the Muslim men but also by many Westerners who constructed their ideas and views of women in the Orient upon the belief that the *harem* is a place where men have sexual access to multiple females (Ahmed, 1982 as cited in Mabro, 1991).

These perceptions of the *harem* and of women as objects of sexuality and desire motivated many Western men to travel to the Orient in order to discover the mysteries of the *harem* and to posses its women. However, the boundaries between the public domain and the private one were impassable barriers. Some of these men confessed that they did not see women during their visits to the Arab Muslim world and most of the written accounts of these travelers retell the stories of local men (Mabro, 1991). Furthermore, the veil was another obstacle to see women when they were outside the private sphere, since women were mostly covered in public. As Alloula once noted: "[T]he first thing the foreign eye catches about Algerian women is that they are concealed from sight" (Alloula, 1986:7).

During the colonial reigns, in contrast to the males who could have the opportunity to seek relationships with local women, white women were not allowed to interact with the natives. They were considered vulnerable to the sexual desires of the colonized men. Hence, they had to be protected and sets of regulations were enacted to control interactions between them and the natives and to limit the freedom of both (Stoler, 1997).

In a way, the female accounts in Dahab in the contemporary time are a continuation of the past. Contrasting historical Western male accounts, recent foreign female experiences in Dahab have shown that they have reproduced these narratives of desire but in modified forms based on the historical context, their gender, as well as their invasion of the public domain that was purely a male domain. Over the past few decades the feminist movement has caused many changes in the lives of women. Women have gained more rights in many areas of life, including their equality with men, and their increased presence in public spheres, which allowed them to work and travel. In addition, the globalization of tourism and the technological advances of transport have given women the opportunities to travel and have experiences that were not available to them in the past. Hence, the perceptions of the Orient do not only include men's perceptions of women but also women in the West have developed stereotypical views about Eastern men. I refer here to the Western women coming to Dahab with preset ideas of Eastern men as oversexed, masculine and exotic beings. Given the fact that the encounters take place in a different era, in the framework of tourism and on a different level in the public domain represented by men, makes it easier for the women to satisfy their fantasies about Eastern men in a context that is linked to power and politics within the framework of global and colonialist histories between Egypt and the West.

Chapter 7
Conclusion

GLOBAL TRENDS, ECONOMIC hardships in addition to social problems in Egypt have left their mark on the Egyptian people in many aspects of their lives. They constitute the main reason for the emergence of a subculture in the tourist destination Dahab similar to many others locally and globally. The tourist businesses in Dahab dominated by underprivileged young men have opened a space for young Egyptian males lacking professional training, to work in the tourist industry. This disenfranchised group who suffers directly from the economic changes in Egypt adopt different strategies for overcoming poverty in which sexuality is used as means to reach their economic goals. In spite of the fact that sexual interactions between Egyptian men and foreign women in Dahab are not based on a fee-per-encounter economic setup, in many cases they carry indirect as well as direct economic benefits to the men involved.

By adopting these behaviors, the men jeopardize their relationship with their families and involve themselves in conflicts with the state represented in the police authorities who try to regulate behaviors considered inappropriate in the Egyptian society.

It has been illustrated how the interactions with foreign women result in changes in the men's views about their culture, their sexuality, and also about the Other. It is out of these views that feelings of alienation from society and traditions are created.

Due to their life-style, many young Egyptian men who work in the tourist industry are vulnerable to diseases, given their limited knowledge about STDs. The ones who do have the knowledge try to repress the existence of diseases by constructing personal understandings of risk and health. Hence, no precautions are usually taken when the men have sexual interactions with foreign women. This is how they become liable to the high risk of contracting diseases, especially in an era where AIDS spreads fast among heterosexual western women who are considered to be the fastest growing AIDS group (Stanton, 1992).

The denial of the existence of disease by the officials who argue that Egyptians are safe from AIDS in particular and STDs in general, is a reflection of a general neglect and lack of awareness within the society, which is also prevalent in the behavior of the young men in Dahab. In most cases, safe sex is not practiced and medical tests for the various STDs are sought only when requested by the foreign women. However, under the influence of drugs and alcohol that are regularly consumed in Dahab, people are often not fully aware of their actions and the implications of their behaviors.

Furthermore, the research reveals how female tourists' accounts in Dahab are part of a post-colonial discourse of "exotification" and "racialization." It explains how these relations differ from their historical context and shows how foreign women come to Dahab to experience facets of femininity and desirability that are not available to them in their own societies, while keeping control of the relationship, their partners, and their sexuality.

Both western females and Egyptian men in Dahab seek emotional and psychological satisfaction that seems to be difficult to experience within their hegemonic cultures. In Egypt, the economic hardships and social problems make it difficult for many men to get married and establish a family, which consequently affects their position as men by not being able to fulfill their normal traditional roles and express their masculinity. In the relationships with foreign women, the men in Dahab play out their masculinity in a different way compared to how they would exhibit it in their hegemonic culture. Taking into consideration the societal background of the men in Dahab, they are being emasculated by gender negotiations with foreign women, since they have been socialized in a male dominated society.

Furthermore, the research illustrates how the female discourses in Dahab show that the relationships with Egyptian men are a means that help them satisfy their fantasies about the "Orient" and Middle Eastern men. Additionally, these interactions give the foreign women the opportunity to enjoy the different, feminized experiences that magnify their femininity and give them a new feeling of desirability. Dunne (2003) argues that gender and sexuality are closely linked and have some common characteristics since they both structure gender relations and regulate masculinities and femininities. Gender is continuously shaped by daily contacts with others, "we *do*

Chapter 7 Conclusion

rather than *have* gender" (Dunne, 2003:59). Hence, foreign female accounts in Dahab illustrate that their experiences are engendered through the sexual encounters they have with Egyptian men. However, the same women practice means of control over their partners, which are acquired and enforced by their economic power. In addition, their experienced "racial superiority" enables them to determine the terms of the relationship with their Egyptian partners. Furthermore, many of them limit their relationship to the geographical place Dahab, which is also considered another means of control to reduce the possibility of risking stigmatization and humiliation in their societies for having relationships with Egyptian men who may be considerably younger than them.

Cultures in cities like Dahab are worth studying since they show how interactions with different cultures have their impact on people's views. They also illustrate how the changes taking place in the Egyptian society lead the people to adopt different strategies to cope with their problems.

The behavioral patterns taking place in Dahab are not limited to this particular place. However, the fact that Dahab is a location where sexual encounters between Egyptian men and foreign tourists can be observed on a large scale and are practiced extensively makes it a unique place, or practically speaking, one of a kind in Egypt due to the absence of societal as well as familial control mechanisms.

Bibliography

Abaza, Mona. 2001. "Perceptions of 'Urfi Marriage in the Egyptian Press," *ISIM Newsletter*, 7:20–21.
Adler, Emily, and Roger Clark. 1999. *How It's Done: An Innovation to Social Research*. New York: Wadsworth Publishing Company.
Ali, Hamid, and Fouad Salim. 1992. *Law Number 10 for the Year 1961 Concerning the Abolishment of Prostitution*. Cairo: The General Authority of Governmental Printhouse.
Ali, Kamran. 1996. "Rethinking Masculinities." In Sondra Zeidenstein and Kirsten Moore, eds., *Learning about Sexuality: A Practical Beginning*. New York: The Population Council.
———. 2002. *Family Planning in Egypt: New Bodies-New Selves*. Austin: University of Texas Press.
Alloula, Malek. 1986. *The Colonial Harem*. Minneapolis: The University of Minnesota Press.
Appadurai, Arjun. 1996. *Modernity at Large: Cultural Dimensions of Globalization*. Minneapolis: University of Minnesota Press.
Bailey, Kenneth. 1982. *Methods of Social Research*. New York: The Free Press.
Bayat, Asef. 2000. "From 'Dangerous Classes' to 'Quiet Rebels': Politics of the Urban Subaltern of the Global South," *International Sociology*, 15(3):533–557.
Behbehanian, Laleh. 2000. "The Production, Performance and Articulation of Masculinity in Dahab, South Sinai." Unpublished Masters Thesis: Sociology/Anthropology/Psychology/Egyptology Department, The American University in Cairo.

Bibliography

Blackman, Winifred S. 1927. *The Fellahin of Upper Egypt*. London: George G. Harrap and Co.
Blumer, Herbert. 1969. *Symbolic Interactionism: Perspective and Method*. New Jersey: Prentice-Hall, Inc.: Englewood Cliffs.
Botman, Selma. 1999. *Engendering Citizenship in Egypt: The History and Society of the Modern Middle East*. New York: Colombia University Press.
Bowman, Glenn. 1989. "Fucking Tourists: Sexual Relations and Tourism in Jerusalem's Old City" *Critique of Anthropology*, 9(2):77–93.
Brandes, Stanley. 1981. "Like Wounded Stages: Male Sexual Ideology in an Andalusian Town". In Sherry B. Ortner and Harriet Whitehead, eds., *Sexual Meaning: The Cultural Construction of Gender and Sexuality*. Cambridge: Cambridge University Press.
Collumbien, Martine and Sarah Hawkes. 2000. "Missing Men's Messages: Does the Reproductive Health Approach Respond to Men's Sexual Health Needs?" Culture, Health & Sexuality, pp. 135–150.
Connell, R.W. 1998. "Masculinities and Globalization" *Men and Masculinities*, 1(1):3–23.
Davidson, Julia O'Connell and Jacqueline Sanchez Taylor. 1999. "Fantasy Islands: Exploring the Demand for Sex Tourism." In Kamala Kempadoo, ed., *Sun, Sex and Gold: Tourism and Sex Work in the Caribbean*. New York: Brown and Littelfield Publishers, INC.
Dixon-Mueller, Ruth. 1996. "The Sexuality Connection in Reproductive Health." In Sondra Zeidenstein and Kirsten Moore, eds., *Learning about Sexuality: A Practical Beginning*. New York: The Population Council.
Dorkenoo, Edfu. 1994. "Cutting the Rose; Female Genital Mutilation: The Practice and its Prevention." Monitory Rights Publications.
Dunne, Gillian A. 2003. "A Passion for 'Sameness'? Sexuality and Gender Accountability." In Jeffrey Weeks, Janet Holland, and Matthew Waites, eds., *Sexuality and Society: A Reader*. Cambridge: Polity Press.
Egypt Focus. 2001. Dahab. http://www.egyptfocus.com/dahab_here.htm. Electronic Document. Visited April 25, 2001 and November 22, 2002.
Foucault, Michel. 1979. *The History of Sexuality: An Introduction*. Vol.1. London: Penguin Books.
Gad El Haq Ali Gad El Haq, with Mohamed Nabil Younis, Ahmed Ragaa Abdel Hamdi Ragab, and Gamal Aboul Serour. 1997. *Ahkam al-Shari'a al-Islamiya fi Masa'el Tebbiya 'an al-Amrad al-Nisa'ya wal-Siha al-Ingabiya*. Cairo: Al-Walid Printhouse.
Geertz, Clifford. 1973. *The Interpretation of Cultures*. New York: Basic Books.
Giddens, Anthony. 1993. *Sociology*. Cambridge: Polity Press.

Gilmore, David D. 2001. "The Manhood Puzzle." In Caroline B. Brettel and Carolyn F. Sargent, eds., *Gender in Cross-Cultural Perspective*. New Jersey: Prentice Hall.

Gilsenan, Michael. 1996. *Lords of the Lebanese Marches: Violence and Narrative in Arab Society*. London and New York: I.B. Tauris Publishers.

Gutmann, Matthew C. 1996. *The Meaning of Macho: Being a Man in Mexico City*. Berkeley: University of California Press.

Herzfeld, Michael. 1985. *The Poetics of Manhood: Contest and Identity in a Cretan Village*. New Jersey: Princeton University Press.

Hoodfar, Homa. 1999. *Between Marriage and the Market: Intimate Policies and Survival in Cairo*. Cairo: The American University in Cairo Press.

Humphreys, Andrew, Siona Jenkins, Leanne Logan, Geert Cole, and Damien Simonis. 1999. *Lonely Planet: Egypt*. Lonely Planet Publications Pty Ltd.

Johnson, Branden B. and Vincent T. Covello, eds. 1987. "Reality, Perception, and the Social Construction of Risk." In *The Social and Cultural Construction of Risk: Essays on Risk Selection and Perception*. Dordrecht, Boston: D. Reidel Publishing Company.

Keddie, Nikkie. 1998. "The New Religious Politics: Where, When and Why Do 'Fundamentalisms' Appear?" *Comparative Studies in Society and History*, 40(4): 696–723.

Khalifa, Ayman. 1995. "The Withering Youth of Egypt." *Ru'ya*, Spring, (7)6–11.

Korayem, Karima. 1997. *Egypt's Economic Reform and Structural Adjustment (ERSAP)*. Cairo: The Egyptian Center for Economic Studies.

Kristeva, Julia. 1986. *The Kristiva Reader*. New York: Colombia University Press.

Lavie, Smadar. 1990. *Poetics of Military Occupation*. California: University of California Press.

Lear, Dana. 1997. *Sex and Sexuality: Risk and Relationships in the Age of AIDS*. London: SAGE Publications.

Levy, Robert and Douglas W. Hollan. 1998. "Person-Centered Interviewing and Observation." In H. Russell Bernard, ed., *Handbook of Methods in Cultural Anthropology*. London: Altamira Press.

Mabro, Judy. 1991. *Veiled Half-truths: Western Travellers' Perceptions of Middle Eastern Women*. London: I.B. Tauris.

MacCannell, Dean. 1999. *The Tourist: A New Theory of the Leisure Class*. Berkeley: University of California Press.

Martin, Emily. 1992. *The Woman in the Body: A Culture Analysis of Reproduction*. Boston: Beacon Press.

Mernissi, Fatma. 1987. *Beyond the Veil: Male-Female Dynamics in Modern Muslim Society*. Indiana University Press.

———. 1991. *Women and Islam: An Historical and Theological Enquiry*. Oxford: Basil Blackwell.

Moore, Henrietta. 1994. *A Passion for Difference: Essays in Anthropology and Gender*. Polity Press.

Ortner, Sherry. 1974. "Is female to Male as Nature Is to Culture?" In Michelle Zimbalist Rosaldo and Louise Lamphere, eds., *Women, Culture and Society*. Stanford: Stanford University Press.

Pateman, Carole. 1988. *The Sexual Contract*. Cambridge: Polity Press.

Philips, Joan L. 1999. "Tourist-Oriented Prostitution in Barbados: The Case of the Beach Boy and the White Female Tourist." In Kamala Kempadoo, ed., *Sex and Gold: Tourism and Sex Work in the Caribbean*. New York: Brown and Littelfield Publishers, INC.

Ryan, Chris and Michael Hall. 2001. *Sex Tourism: Marginal People and Liminalities*. London: Routledge.

Ritzer, George. 1996. *Sociological Theory*. New York: MacGraw-Hill Companies, Inc.

Rugh, Andrea. 1988. *Family in Contemporary Egypt*. Cairo: The American University in Cairo Press.

Said, Edward W. 1978. *Orientalism: Western Conceptions of the Orient*. Penguin Books.

Sanchez Taylor, Jacqueline. 2001. "Dollars Are a Girl's Best Friend? Female Tourists' Sexual Behaviour in the Caribbean", *Sociology*, 35(3):749–764.

Shohat, Ella, and Robert Stam. 1994. *Unthinking Eurocentrism: Multiculturalism and the Media*. London and New York: Routledge.

Smith, Carol A. 1994. "Race/Class/Gender Ideology in Guatemala." In Brackette F Williams, ed., *Women Out of Place: The Gender of Agency and the Race of Nationality* New York: Routledge.

Stanton, Donna C. 1992. *Discourses of Sexuality: From Aristotle to AIDS*. Ann Arbor: University of Michigan Press.

Stoler, Ann Laura. 1995. *Race and the Education of Desire: Foucault's History of Sexuality and the Colonial Order of Things*. Durham: Duke University Press.

Stoler, Ann Laura. 1997. *Making Empire Respectable: The Politics of Race and Sexual Morality in Twentieth-Century Colonial Cultures*. London: The University of Minnesota Press.

Wassif, Nadia and Abdalla Mansour. 1999. *Investigating Masculinities and Female Genital Mutilation in Egypt*. Cairo: National NGO Center for Population and Development.

Waters, Malcolm. 1995. *Globalization*. London: Routledge.

Wysocki, Diane Kholos. 2001. *Reading in Social Research Methods*. Canada: Wadsworth.

About the Author

MUSTAFA ABDALLA is a lecturer in Anthropology and a Ph.D. candidate at the Free University of Berlin. This research is based on his MA thesis at the Sociology/Anthropology Department, the American University in Cairo. The thesis won the Magda al-Nowaihi Award for Gender Studies at AUC.

CAIRO PAPERS IN SOCIAL SCIENCE

Volume One 1977–1978
1 *Women, Health and Development, Cynthia Nelson, ed.
2 *Democracy in Egypt, Ali E. Hillal Dessouki, ed.
3 *Mass Communications and the October War, Olfat Hassan Agha
4 *Rural Resettlement in Egypt, Helmy Tadros
5 *Saudi Arabian Bedouin, Saad E. Ibrahim and Donald P. Cole

Volume Two 1978–1979
1 *Coping With Poverty in a Cairo Community, Andrea B. Rugh
2 *Modernization of Labor in the Arab Gulf, Enid Hill
3 Studies in Egyptian Political Economy, Herbert M. Thompson
4 *Law and Social Change in Contemporary Egypt, Cynthia Nelson and Klaus Friedrich Koch, eds.
5 *The Brain Drain in Egypt, Saneya Saleh

Volume Three 1979–1980
1 *Party and Peasant in Syria, Raymond Hinnebusch
2 *Child Development in Egypt, Nicholas V. Ciaccio
3 *Living Without Water, Asaad Nadim et. al.
4 *Export of Egyptian School Teachers, Suzanne A. Messiha
5 *Population and Urbanization in Morocco, Saad E. Ibrahim

Volume Four 1980–1981
1 *Cairo's Nubian Families, Peter Geiser
2, 3 *Symposium on Social Research for Development: Proceedings, Social Research Center
4 *Women and Work in the Arab World, Earl L. Sullivan and Karima Korayem

Volume Five 1982
1 *Ghagar of Sett Guiranha: A Study of a Gypsy Community in Egypt, Nabil Sobhi Hanna
2 *Distribution of Disposal Income and the Impact of Eliminating Food Subsidies in Egypt, Karima Korayem
3 *Income Distribution and Basic Needs in Urban Egypt, Amr Mohie el-Din

Volume Six 1983
1 *The Political Economy of Revolutionary Iran, Mihssen Kadhim

2   *Urban Research Strategies in Egypt, Richard A. Lobban, ed.
3   *Non-alignment in a Changing World, Mohammed el-Sayed Selim, ed.
4   *The Nationalization of Arabic and Islamic Education in Egypt: Dar al-Alum and al-Azhar, Lois A. Arioan

Volume Seven 1984

1   *Social Security and the Family in Egypt, Helmi Tadros
2   *Basic Needs, Inflation and the Poor of Egypt, Myrette el-Sokkary
3   *The Impact of Development Assistance On Egypt, Earl L. Sullivan, ed.
4   *Irrigation and Society in Rural Egypt, Sohair Mehanna, Richard Huntington and Rachad Antonius

Volume Eight 1985

1, 2   *Analytic Index of Survey Research in Egypt, Madiha el-Safty, Monte Palmer and Mark Kennedy

Volume Nine 1986

1   *Philosophy, Ethics and Virtuous Rule, Charles E. Butterworth
2   The 'Jihad': An Islamic Alternative in Egypt, Nemat Guenena
3   *The Institutionalization of Palestinian Identity in Egypt, Maha A. Dajani
4   *Social Identity and Class in a Cairo Neighborhood, Nadia A. Taher

Volume Ten 1987

1   *Al-Sanhuri and Islamic Law, Enid Hill
2   *Gone For Good, Ralph Sell
3   *The Changing Image of Women in Rural Egypt, Mona Abaza
4   *Informal Communities in Cairo: the Basis of a Typology, Linda Oldham, Haguer el Hadidi, Hussein Tamaa

Volume Eleven 1988

1   *Participation and Community in Egyptian New Lands: the Case of South Tahrir, Nicholas Hopkins et. al.
2   Palestinian Universities Under Occupation, Antony T. Sullivan
3   Legislating Infitah: Investment, Foreign Trade and Currency Laws, Khaled M. Fahmy
4   Social History of An Agrarian Reform Community in Egypt, Reem Saad

Volume Twelve 1989

1   *Cairo's Leap Forward: People, Households and Dwelling Space, Fredric Shorter
2   *Women, Water and Sanitation: Household Water Use in Two Egyptian Villages, Samiha el-Katsha et. al.

3   Palestinian Labor in a Dependent Economy: Women Workers in the West Bank Clothing Industry, Randa Siniora
4   The Oil Question in Egyptian-Israeli Relations, 1967–1979: A Study in International Law and Resource Politics, Karim Wissa

Volume Thirteen 1990
1   *Squatter Markets in Cairo, Helmi R. Tadros, Mohamed Feteeha, Allen Hibbard
2   *The Sub-culture of Hashish Users in Egypt: A Descriptive Analytic Study, Nashaat Hassan Hussein
3   *Social Background and Bureaucratic Behavior in Egypt, Earl L. Sullivan, el Sayed Yassin, Ali Leila, Monte Palmer
4   *Privatization: the Egyptian Debate, Mostafa Kamel el-Sayyid

Volume Fourteen 1991
1   *Perspectives on the Gulf Crisis, Dan Tschirgi and Bassam Tibi
2   *Experience and Expression: Life Among Bedouin Women in South Sinai, Deborah Wickering
3   Impact of Temporary International Migration on Rural Egypt, Atef Hanna Nada
4   *Informal Sector in Egypt, Nicholas S. Hopkins ed.

Volume Fifteen, 1992
1   *Scenes of Schooling: Inside a Girls' School in Cairo, Linda Herrera
2   Urban Refugees: Ethiopians and Eritreans in Cairo, Dereck Cooper
3   Investors and Workers in the Western Desert of Egypt: An Exploratory Survey, Naeim Sherbiny, Donald Cole, Nadia Makary
4   *Environmental Challenges in Egypt and the World, Nicholas S. Hopkins, ed.

Volume Sixteen, 1993
1   *The Socialist Labor Party: A Case Study of a Contemporary Egyptian Opposition Party, Hanaa Fikry Singer
2   *The Empowerment of Women: Water and Sanitation Iniatives in Rural Egypt, Samiha el Katsha, Susan Watts
3   The Economics and Politics of Structural Adjustment in Egypt: Third Annual Symposium
4   *Experiments in Community Development in a Zabbaleen Settlement, Marie Assaad and Nadra Garas

Volume Seventeen, 1994
1   Democratization in Rural Egypt: A Study of the Village Local Popular Council, Hanan Hamdy Radwan

2   *Farmers and Merchants: Background for Structural Adjustment in Egypt*, Sohair Mehanna, Nicholas S. Hopkins and Bahgat Abdelmaksoud
3   *Human Rights: Egypt and the Arab World, Fourth Annual Symposium*
4   *Environmental Threats in Egypt: Perceptions and Actions*, Salwa S. Gomaa, ed.

Volume Eighteen, 1995

1   *Social Policy in the Arab World*, Jacqueline Ismael & Tareq Y. Ismael
2   *Workers, Trade Union and the State in Egypt: 1984–1989*, Omar el-Shafie
3   *The Development of Social Science in Egypt: Economics, History and Sociology; Fifth Annual Symposium*
4   *Structural Adjustment, Stabilization Policies and the Poor in Egypt*, Karima Korayem

Volume Nineteen, 1996

1   *Nilopolitics: A Hydrological Regime, 1870–1990*, Mohamed Hatem el-Atawy
2   **Images of the Other: Europe and the Muslim World Before 1700*, David R. Blanks et al.
3   **Grass Roots Participation in the Development of Egypt*, Saad Eddin Ibrahim et al.
4   *The Zabbalin Community of Muqattam*, Elena Volpi and Doaa Abdel Motaal

Volume Twenty, 1997

1   *Class, Family and Power in an Egyptian Village*, Samer el-Karanshawy
2   *The Middle East and Development in a Changing World*, Donald Heisel, ed.
3   *Arab Regional Women's Studies Workshop*, Cynthia Nelson and Soraya Altorki, eds.
    "Just a Gaze": Female Clientele of Diet Clinics in Cairo: an Ethnomedical Study, Iman Farid Bassyouny

Volume Twenty-one, 1998

1   *Turkish Foreign Policy During the Gulf War of 1990–1991*, Mostafa Aydin
2   *State and Industrial Capitalism in Egypt*, Samer Soliman
3   *Twenty Years of Development in Egypt (1977–1997): Part I*, Mark C. Kennedy
4   *Twenty Years of Development in Egypt (1977–1997): Part II*, Mark C. Kennedy

Volume Twenty-two, 1999

1   *Poverty and Poverty Alleviation Strategies in Egypt*, Ragui Assaad and Malak Rouchdy
2   *Between Field and Text: Emerging Voices in Egyptian Social Science*, Seteney Shami and Linda Hererra, eds.
3   *Masters of the Trade: Crafts and Craftspeople in Cairo, 1750–1850*, Pascale Ghazaleh
4   *Discourses in Contemporary Egypt: Politics and Social Issues*, Enid Hill, ed.

Volume Twenty-three, 2000

1   *Fiscal Policy Measures in Egypt: Public Debt and Food Subsidy,* Gouda Abdel-Khalek and Karima Korayem
2   *New Frontiers in the Social History of the Middle East,* Enid Hill, ed.
3   *Egyptian Encounters,* Jason Thompson, ed.
4   *Women's Perception of Environmental Change in Egypt,* Eman el Ramly

Volume Twenty-four, 2001

1, 2   *The New Arab Family,* Nicholas S. Hopkins, ed.
3   *An Investigation of the Phenomenon of Polygyny in Rural Egypt,* Laila S. Shahd
4   *The Terms of Empowerment: Islamic Women Activists in Egypt,* Sherine Hafez

Volume Twenty-five, 2002

1, 2   *Elections in the Middle East: What do they Mean?* Iman A. Hamdy, ed.
3   *Employment Crisis of Female Graduates in Egypt: An Ethnographic Account,* Ghada F. Barsoum
4   *Palestinian and Israeli Nationalism: Identity Politics and Education in Jerusalem,* Evan S. Weiss

Volume Twenty-six, 2003

1   *Culture and Natural Environment: Ancient and Modern Middle Eastern Texts,* Sharif S. Elmusa, ed.
2   *Street Children in Egypt: Group Dynamics and Subcultural Constituents,* Nashaat Hussein
3   *IMF–Egyptian Debt Negotiations,* Bessma Momani
4   *Forced Migrants and Host Societies in Egypt and Sudan,* Fabienne Le Houérou

Volume Twenty-seven, 2004

1&2   *Cultural Dynamics in Contemporary Egypt,* Maha Abdelrahman, Iman A. Hamdy, Malak Rouchdy and Reem Saad (eds.)
3   *The Role of Local Councils in Empowerment and Poverty Reduction,* Solava Ibrahim

* currently out of print

ملخص

تهدف هذه الدراسة الانثروبولوجية الى تحليل الاستراتيجيات التى يتبناها الشباب العامل فى مجال السياحة الغير رسمى فى مدينة دهب لمواجهة التغييرات الاجتماعية والظروف الاقتصادية الصعبة التى نتجت عن سياسة التحرر الاقتصادى والخصخصة التى اتبعتها الحكومة المصرية فى العقود الاخيرة. هذه الظروف كانت لها آثارعديدة على المجتمع المصرى من أهمها نقص فرص العمل وارتفاع سن الزواج بين الشباب نظراً لعدم قدرة الكثير منهم تحمل التكاليف المتزايدة للزواج.

فى هذا الاطار، تتطرق الدراسة الى قضية الزواج العرفى المنتشر بشكل ملحوظ فى دهب بين الشباب المصرى وكثيرات من السائحات الاجنبيات والذى يلجأ اليه الشباب من أجل الحصول على مزايا مادية وايضاً كوسيلة للسفر الى الخارج للبحث عن فرص عمل أفضل. كما تتعرض ايضاً الى العلاقات الجنسية التى يقيمها الشباب معهن بالإضافة الى موضوع السياحة الجنسية والنتائج المترتبة على تبنى الشباب لسلوكيات غير شائعة فى المجتمع والتى تؤدى بدورها الى حدوث العديد من المشكلات بين هؤلاء الشباب من ناحية وكل من أسرهم والسلطات الأمنية من ناحية أخرى.

وعلى جانب آخر، تتناول الدراسة الاسباب التى تجذب الشباب المصرى والسائحات الاجنبيات الى دهب حيث تلقى الضوء على آراء السيدات الاجنبيات فى العلاقات التى يقيمنها فى دهب وعلى عدم رضائهن عن تأثير الحركة النسائية فى الغرب على وضعهن كسيدات فى المجتمعات الغربية.

وأخيراً، تربط هذه الدراسة بين العلاقات التى تحدث فى دهب فى الوقت الحاضر بين الشباب المصرى والسيدات الغربيات والعلاقات التاريخية بين الشرق والغرب من منظور تاريخى.

حقوق النشر محفوظة لقسم النشر بالجامعة الامريكية بالقاهرة
١١٣ شارع قصر العيني، القاهرة - مصر
طبعة أولى: ٢٠٠٧

جميع الحقوق محفوظة. ممنوع اعادة طبع أى جزء من الكتاب أو حفظه بعد تصحيحه أو نقله فى أية صورة أو بأية واسطة الكترونية أو ميكانيكية أو تصويرية أو تسجيلية أو غير ذلك بدون اتصريح المسبق من صاحب حق النشر.

صورة الغلاف: متزى بايز – دهب

رقم دار الكتب: ٠٥/٢٣٧٥٠
الترقيم الدولى: ٤ ٠١٣ ٤١٦ ٩٧٧ ٩٧٨

بحوث القاهرة
فى العلوم الاجتماعية

مجلد ٢٧   عدد ٤   شتاء ٢٠٠٤

السياحة وعلاقات الشواطىء في دهب

مصطفى عبد الله

قسم النشر بالجامعة الامريكية بالقاهرة
القاهرة نيويورك